R.N. COUDENHOVE KALERGI

PRACTICAL IDEALISM

NOBILITY – TECHNOLOGY - PACIFISM

RICHARD NIKOLAUS COUDENHOVE-KALERGI
(1894-1972)

PRACTICAL IDEALISM
NOBILITY – TECHNOLOGY – PACIFISM

Translated by: Dimitra Ekmektsis

PRAKTISCHER IDEALISMUS
ADEL - TECHNIK – PAZIFISMUS

First edition in 1925 by
PANEUROPA – VERLAG - WIEN-LEIPZIG

Published by
OMNIA VERITAS LTD

www.omnia-veritas.com

Dedication

For Kenny

FOREWORD

Practical Idealism is heroism; practical materialism is eudemonism. Those who not believe in ideals have no reason to act ideally; or to fight or suffer for ideals. Because they know and acknowledge only one value: pleasure; only a single evil: pain.

Heroism necessitates faith and commitment to the ideal: the conviction that there are higher values than pleasure and greater evil than pain.

This contradiction runs through the whole of human history; it is the difference between the epicureans and stoics. This difference is much greater than that between theists and atheists: because there were Epicureans who believed in gods, as Epicurus himself; and there were Idealists who were atheists, like Buddha.

So, this is not about believing in gods—but about believing in values. Materialism is unconditional—but unimaginative and uncreative; idealism is always problematic and is often entangled with nonsense and insanity: nevertheless, humanity owes its greatest works and deeds to it.

Heroism is the nobility of ethos. Heroism is as closely related to the aristocratic ideal, as materialism is to the democratic. Even democracy believes more in numbers than in value, more in luck than in greatness. Therefore, political democracy can only become fruitful and creative when it destroys the pseudo-aristocracy of name and of wealth, and eternally gives birth to a new aristocracy of mind and ethos.

The ultimate point of political democracy therefore is: spiritual democracy; it wants to create enjoyment for the materialists, and power for the idealists.

The leader shall replace the ruler—the noble spirit shall replace the noble name—the rich heart shall replace the rich pocket. That is the meaning of progress which is called democracy.

Any other meaning would be cultural suicide.

Therefore, it is no coincidence that Plato, the prophet of the intellectual aristocracy was at the same time the father of the socialist economy; and also, the father of the idealistic world view.

For both, aristocracy and socialism, are practical idealism.

The ascetic idealism of the South manifested itself in religion; the heroic idealism of the North in technology.

Because nature in the North was a challenge to people. Other tribes succumbed; the Europeans accepted the challenge and fought. They fought until they were strong enough to subdue the earth: they fought until they forced the very nature which had challenged them, to serve them.

This fight demanded heroism, and begot heroism. So, for Europe the hero became what the saint was for Asia; hero worship complemented the worship of saints.

The ideal of action took the place of the ideal of devotion, and it was considered greater to fight for an ideal than to suffer.

The meaning of this heroic world mission has only been grasped by Europe in modern times; for it is only with modern times that its technological age—the liberation war against winter—begins. This technological age is also the age of labor. The worker is the hero of our age; his opposite is not the citizen, but the freeloader. The goal of the worker is—to create, that of the freeloader—to consume.

Therefore, technology is modern heroism and the worker is a practical idealist.

The political and social problem of the 20th century is: catching up with the technological progress of the 19th century. This challenge of the times is exceedingly difficult because technology continues developing at a faster pace than the development of man and mankind. This danger can either be averted by slowing technological progress, or by accelerating social progress. Otherwise, humanity will lose its balance and capsize. The World War was a warning. Technology gives humanity a choice: suicide or agreement.

The development of the world in the coming decades will be without precedent. The current imbalance of technological and social organization will either lead to destructive catastrophes—or to political development, that quickly and thoroughly leaves all past models behind and opens a new page in human history.

Since technology makes new paths for the human momentum and for heroism, the war is beginning to play its historical role in human consciousness. Its successor is work. Mankind will organize one day, and wrest from the earth everything that she denies us today. As soon as this concept is realized, every war will be a civil war and every kill a murder. The age of war will then seem just as barbaric as today the age cannibalism.

This development will happen if we believe in it and fight for it; if we are neither so short-sighted as to lose sight of the development—nor so far-sighted as to overlook the practical paths and obstacles that lie between us and our goals: if we are clear-sighted and clearly know how to overcome the upcoming struggles and difficulties with our heroic will.

Only this optimism of the will can complete and defeat the pessimism of knowledge.

Instead of remaining in the grip of the outdated present and dreaming of better opportunities, we want to take an active part in the development of the world through practical idealism.

Vienna,

November 1925

NOBILITY—1920

In memory of my father,
Dr. Heinrich Count Coudenhove-Kalergi
in admiration and gratitude

PART ONE

OF RURAL AND URBAN MEN

1. RURAL MAN—URBANITE

Country and city are the two poles of human existence. Country and city produce their special human: the rural and urban person.

Rural and an urban people are psychological opposites. Farmers of different areas resemble each other emotionally often more than they resemble the people in the neighboring city. Between farm and farm, between city and city is space—between city and farm is time. Among European rural people live the representatives of every age: from the Stone Age to the Middle Ages, while only the metropolitan cities of the Occident, which produced the most extreme urban type, are representative of modern civilization. Centuries, often millennia, separate the big city from the farmland that surrounds it.

The urban man thinks differently, judges differently, feels differently, acts differently than the rural man. Big city life is abstract, mechanical, rational—rural life is concrete, organic, irrational. The urbanite is rational, skeptical, critical—the rural man is emotional, religious, superstitious.

Everything rural man thinks and feels focuses around nature; he lives in symbiosis with the animal, the living creature of God; he is one with his landscape, dependent on weather and season. The focal point of the urban soul, on the other hand, is society; he lives in symbiosis with machines, the dead creations of men; through them, the urban man makes himself as independent as possible from time and space, season and climate.

The rural man believes in the force of nature over man—the urban man believes in the force of man over nature. The rural man is a natural product, the urban man a social product; one sees purpose, measure and goal of the world in the cosmos, the other in humanity.

Rural man is as conservative as nature itself—urban man as progressive as society. All progress is based on cities and city people. The city dweller himself is usually a product of a revolution within a generation that broke with its rural tradition, moved to the big city and started living there on a new basis.

The city robs its inhabitants of the enjoyment of nature's beauty; as compensation it offers them the arts. Theater, concerts, galleries are surrogates for the eternal and changing beauty of the landscape. After a day's work full of ugliness, these art institutes offer urbanites beauty in concentrated form. In the country they are redundant. Nature is the extensive, art the intensive manifestation of beauty.

The relationship between urban man and nature, which he lacks, is ruled by yearning; while nature is always fulfilling the rural man. Therefore, urban man perceives it as romantic, rural man as classic. Social (Christian) moral is an urban phenomenon: because it is a function of human coexistence, of society. The typical city dweller combines

Christian morality with his irreligious skepticism, rationalistic materialism and mechanical atheism. The resulting world view is Socialism: the modern religion of the modern city.

Christianity is little more than a reinterpretation of paganism with altered mythology and new superstition for the rural barbarians of Europe; -a true religion is the belief in nature, in power, in fate.

Urban and rural people do not know each other; therefore, they mistrust and misunderstand each other and live in veiled or open hostility. There are many catchwords under which this basic opposition hides: red and green internationalism; industrialism and agrarianism; progress and reaction; Judaism and Anti-Semitism.

All cities draw their strength from the country; the country draws its culture from the city. The country is the soil from which the cities renew themselves; the source that feeds them; the root from which they flourish. Cities grow and die: the country is eternal.

2. JUNKER—WRITER

The glory of the rural man is the nobleman, the junker. The glory of the urban man is the intellectual, the writer.

Both country and city have sired their specific nobility: noble will versus noble spirit, noble blood versus noble mind. The typical junker combines a maximum of character with a minimum of intellect—the typical writer a maximum of intellect with a minimum of character.

Not always and everywhere lacked the nobleman intellect, or the intellectual character; as in modern England, in the time of minnesingers blood nobility was an outstanding cultural element in Germany; while on the other hand, the Catholic nobility of the Jesuits and the Chinese nobility of the Mandarins proved to have as much character as intellect in their heyday.

The gap between rural and urban people peaks in the junker and the writer. The junker's typical occupation is officer; the typical occupation of the intellectual is journalist.

The junker-officer remained, psychologically and mentally, at the level of knight. Hard on himself and others, dutiful, energetic, steadfast, conservative and narrow-minded, he lives in a world of dynastic, militaristic, national and social prejudices. With a deep mistrust of everything modern, against the big city, democracy, socialism, globalism, he has a deep belief in blood type, in honor, and the world-view of his fathers. He despises the urbanites, especially the Jewish writers.

The writer rushes ahead of his time; without prejudice he represents modern ideas in politics, art, science. He is progressive, skeptical, witty, versatile, mutable; he is a eudaemonist, rationalist, socialist, materialist. He overestimates the mind, underestimates the body and character: and therefore, he despises the junker as a backward barbarian.

The nature of the junker is strength of will—the nature of the writer is agility of the mind. Junker and writer are born rivals and enemies: when the noble class rules, intellect must yield to violence; in such reactionary times, political influence of the intellectuals is switched off, or at least limited. When the intellectual class rules, violence must yield to the mind: democracy triumphs over feudalism, socialism over militarism.

The hatred of the aristocracy of the will and the aristocracy of the mind in Germany is rooted on misunderstanding. Each one sees only the shadowy side of the other and is blind to their virtues. The soul of the rural aristocrat remains forever hidden even from high-ranking intellectuals; while the soul of the urban writer remains alien to almost all aristocrats. Instead of learning from each other, a young lieutenant looks down on the leading minds of modern literature with disdain, while the worst journalist feels only contempt for outstanding officers. First, through this double misunderstanding, militarist Germans underestimated the resistance of the urban masses against the war, and then the revolutionary Germans underestimated the resistance of the rural masses against the revolution. The rural leaders misjudged the psyche of the rural men and their tendency toward reactionism: so, Germany first lost the war, then the revolution.

This difference between the rural and urban man is the fact that both types are extremes, and not to top of blood- and mind-aristocracy. For, the highest manifestation of the blood-aristocracy is the distinguished gentleman; that of the mind-aristocracy is the genius. These two aristocrats are not only compatible, they are related. Caesar, the perfect grand seigneur, was also the most brilliant Roman; Goethe, the peak of genius, was the ultimate grand seigneur of all the German poets. Here, as everywhere, the middle classes diverge the most, while the upper classes are identical.

The ideal aristocrat is at the same time nobility of the will and mind, but neither junker nor writer. He combines world view with willpower, judgement with action, mind with character. If such synthetic personalities do not exist, the divergent aristocrats of the will and the mind should complement each other instead of fighting each other. In Egypt, India, Chaldea, priests and kings (intellectuals and warriors) once ruled together. The priest yielded to the power of the will, the kings to the power of the mind: minds showed the way, arms made the way.

3. GENTLEMEN—BOHEMIAN

Europe's blood- and mind-nobility created each their specific type of person: England's blood-aristocrats created the gentleman; France's mind-aristocrat is the bohemian.

Gentleman and bohemian meet in an effort to escape the desolate ugliness of their bourgeois existence: the gentleman achieves it through style, the bohemian through temperament. The gentleman gives form to formless fife—the bohemian gives color to colorless life.

The gentleman brings order into the chaos of relationships—the bohemian brings freedom.

The beauty ideal of the gentleman is based on form, style, and harmony; it is static, classic, Apollonian. The beauty ideal of the bohemian is based on temperament, freedom, vitality: it is dynamic, romantic, Dionysian.

The gentleman idealizes and stylizes his wealth—the bohemian idealizes and stylizes his poverty.

The gentleman is set on tradition, the bohemian on protest. The essence of the gentleman is conservative, the essence of the bohemian is revolutionary. The mother of the "gentleman-ideal" is England, Europe's most conservative nation. The cradle of "bohemianism" is France, Europe's most revolutionary nation.

The gentleman-ideal points beyond England, back to the Roman stoicism—the bohemia-ideal points beyond France back to the Greek agora. The Roman statesmen are like the gentleman-type—the Greek philosophers the bohemia-type; Caesar and Seneca were gentlemen, Socrates and Diogenes were bohemians.

The focus of the gentleman is physical-psychological—the focus of the bohemian is spiritual; the gentleman may be a fool, the bohemian a criminal.

Both ideals are human crystallization phenomena; as the crystal can only form itself in an unstable environment, so do both owe their existence to the freedoms in England and France.

In imperial Germany this atmosphere of crystallization of personalities was missing: therefore, it could not develop such an ideal. The German lacked the style of the gentleman, the temperament of the bohemian, and the grace and smoothness of both.

Since the German could not find in his reality any form of ideal lifestyle, he sought the German essence in poetry; as physical-psychological ideal he found young Siegfried, as spiritual ideal he found old Faust.

Both ideals were romantic and untimely: in a distortion of reality, the romantic Siegfried-ideal became the Prussian officer, the lieutenant—the romantic Faust-ideal became the German scholar, the professor. Instead of organic, they were mechanical ideals: the officer represents the mechanization of the psyche: the mechanical Siegfried; the professor the mechanical Faust.

Wilhelm's Germany was prouder of its officers and professors than of any other class. In these, it saw the glory of the nation, like England in its political leaders, and like the Roman nations saw in their artists.

If the German nation wants to evolve, it must revise its ideals: its energy must go beyond militaristic one-sidedness and widen to include political-social diversity; its mind must go beyond the purely scientific and widen to synthesize the "poet-thinker".

The 19th century gave the German people two men of greatest style, who embodied these aspirations for a higher *Germanness*: Bismarck, the hero of action; Goethe, the hero of the mind.

Bismarck renews, deepens and animates the corny Siegfried ideal—Goethe renews, deepens and animates the dusty Faust ideal.

Bismarck possessed the positive qualities of the German officer—without his flaws; Goethe possessed the qualities of the educated German—without his flaws. In Bismarck, the superiority of the statesman overcomes the limited nature of the officer—in Goethe the superiority of the poet-thinker overcomes the limits of the intellectual: in both the organic personality ideal overcomes the mechanical, the man overcomes the puppet.

Through his exemplary personality, Bismarck has done more for the development of Germanness than by founding the *Reich* (Empire); through his lofty (Olympian) existence, Goethe has given his country more than with his *Faust*: because *Faust* is, like *Goetz, Werther, Meister* and *Tasso*, merely a fragment in Goethe's being.

Germany should, however, be careful not to mess up and pull down these two ideals by making them too common: not make a sergeant of Bismarck, and a schoolmaster of Goethe.

Germany could grow and heal as a result of these two German geniuses; it could learn from them active and contemplative greatness, productivity, and wisdom. For Bismarck and Goethe are the two focal points around which a new German lifestyle could emerge, which would be equal to Western ideals.

4. INBREEDING—CROSSBREEDING

Usually, the rural man is a product of inbreeding, the urban man a mixed breed.

The parents and grandparents of a farmer usually come from the same, sparsely-populated area; the nobleman comes from the same sparse upper class of the same sparsely-populated area. In both cases, the ancestors are related to each other by blood, and are therefore physically, psychologically and mentally similar. As a result, they pass on to their children and descendants their common traits, tendencies of will, passions, prejudices and inhibitions to an even greater degree. The essential features resulting from such inbreeding are: loyalty, piety, sense of family and caste, consistency, stubbornness, vigor, close-mindedness; more prejudices, less objectivity, and a narrow horizon. Here is a generation that is not a variation of the previous, but simply a duplication. Conservation in place of evolution.

In the big city, races and classes meet. As a rule, urbanites are miscegenational (mixed-race), and from various social and national groups. In them, the character traits, prejudices, inhibitions, tendencies of will, and world views of their parents and grandparents are eliminated, or at least weakened. The result is that mixed-breeds often supplement their lack of character, lack of inhibitions, weakness of will, inconsistency, impiety and disloyalty with objectivity, versatility, mental restlessness, freedom from prejudices and a broader horizon. Mixed-breeds are always different from their parents and grandparents; each generation is a variation of the previous one, either in terms of evolution or degeneration.

The inbred man is always a one-soul person—the mixed-breed man a multi-soul person. In each individual, his ancestors live on as elements of his soul: if they resemble each other, his soul is uniform; if they are diverse, the man is diverse, complicated, distinct.

The size of a mind lies in its extensiveness, that is, in its ability to grasp and to embrace everything; the size of a character depends on its depth, that is, in its ability to will, intently and single-mindedly. In a certain sense, wisdom and restlessness are contradictory.

The more pronounced the ability and tendency of a person is to wisely see things from all sides and without prejudice—the weaker usually his will to act impulsively and biased: because every motive is questioned by a counter-motive, every belief by skepticism, and every action by the understanding of its cosmic insignificance. Only the biased, single-minded man can be effective. But there is not only an unconscious, naïve narrow-mindedness, but also a conscious, heroic narrow-mindedness. The heroic single-minded man—and to this type belong all truly great men of action—from time to time switches off all the sides of his being, except the one required for his action. He can be objective, critical, skeptical, and mindful before or after the action, but he is subjective, faithful, narrow-minded and unfair during the action.

Wisdom inhibits action—action denies wisdom. The strongest will is ineffective if it has no direction; even a weak will triggers the strongest effect, if it is focused.

There is no life of action without wrong-doing, error, guilt: who is afraid of animosity, stays in the realm of thought, tranquility, passivity. Truthful people are always silent: because every assertion is, in a certain sense, a lie, a sin; pure-hearted people are always inactive, because every action is, in a sense, wrong. But it is brave to speak at the risk of lying; to act at the risk of wrongdoing.

Inbreeding strengthens the character, but weakens the mind. Miscegenation weakens the character, but strengthens the mind. When inbreeding and race mixing are favorable, they result in the highest human type, combining the strongest character with the sharpest of minds. Where inbreeding and race mixing are unfavorable, they result in a degenerate type with weak character and dull mind.

The man of the future will be a mixed-breed. Today's races and castes will fall victim to the increased overcoming of space, time and prejudice. The Eurasian-Negroid race of the future, similar in its features to the ancient Egyptians, will replace the diversity of nations with a diversity of "personalities". According to heredity laws, variety of the descendants grows out of the variety of the ancestors, and uniformity of descendants out of uniformity of the ancestors. In single-race families, one child resembles the other: because all represent one common family type. In mixed-race families the children look different from each other: each forms a new variation of the diverse parental and ancestral elements.

Inbreeding produces a characteristic type—race mixing produces original personalities.

The predecessor of the planetary race of the future in modern Europe is the Russian, as a Slavic-, Tatarian-, and Finnish mixed breed; because he, among all European nationals, has the least amount of any race, and he is the typical multi-soul person with a wide, rich, all-encompassing soul.

His strongest opposite is the isolated Brit, the highly inbred one-soul person, whose strength lies in character, will, and in the typical. Modern Europe owes to him the most reserved, most complete type: the gentleman.

5. HEATHEN AND CHRISTIAN MENTALITY

Two types of souls compete for world domination: paganism and Christianity. With the denominations that carry these names, these souls have only superficial relationships with the denominations that carry these names. If the emphasis is shifted from the dogmatic to the ethical, and from mythological to psychological, Buddhism is transformed into Ultra-Christianity, whereas "Americanism" appears as modernized paganism. The Orient is the main bearer of Christian, the Occident the main bearer of pagan mentality; the Chinese pagans are better Christians than the Christian Germans.

Paganism places energy, Christianity love at the top of the ethical scale. The Christian ideal is the loving saint, the pagan ideal the victorious hero. Christianity wants to transform the homo ferus into a homo domesticus, and the predator-human into the pet-human, whereas paganism wants to make man "superhuman". Christianity wants to tame a lion to be a house cat—paganism to raise a cat to be a tiger.

The main herald of modern Christianity was Tolstoi; the main preacher of modern paganism, Nietzsche.

The old Germanic religion was pure paganism. It lived on under a Christian mask: In the Middle Ages as chivalry, in modern times as imperialist and militaristic ideology. Officers, junkers, colonists and captains of industry are the leading representatives of modern-day paganism. Drive, bravery, greatness, freedom, power, fame and honor: these are the ideals of paganism; whereas love, gentleness, humility, compassion, and self-denial are Christian ideals. The antithesis: paganism—Christianity does not coincide with the antithesis: rural—urban, nor with: inbreeding—race mixing. But doubtless, rural barbarianism and inbreeding favor the development of a pagan civilization, and race mixing the development of a Christian mentality.

Generally, pagan individualism is only possible in sparsely populated parts of the earth, where the individual can flourish and unfold recklessly, without immediately antagonizing his fellow humans. In overpopulated areas, where people live in close proximity to each other, the social principal of mutual support must complement and, in part supersede the individual struggle for survival.

Christianity and socialism are cosmopolitan products. Christianity, as a world religion, took its starting point in the diverse cosmopolitan city of Rome; socialism from the multi-national industrial cities of the occident. Both manifestations of Christian mentality are based on internationalism. The resistance to Christianity emanated from the rural populations (pagans); just as today, the rural population is the strongest resistance to the realization of a socialist way of living.

Sparsely populated, northern areas were always the centers of pagan willpower, and densely populated, southern areas were sites of Christian sentiment. Where today there is talk of the difference between Eastern and Western spirituality, it usually means nothing else but the difference between the people of the south and the north. The Japanese, as the northernmost Oriental, is often more "Occidental"; while the mentality of Southern Italians and South Americans is more "Oriental". For the state of the soul, the latitude seems to be more decisive than the degree of longitude.

Not only the geographical location: but the historical development has a determining influence on the soul of a nation. The Chinese, as well as the Jews, feel more Christians than the Germanic nations, because their cultures are older. Germanic people are closer in time to primitive man than the Chinese or the Jews; these two ancient civilizations were able to emancipate themselves more thoroughly from the pagan-natural way of life because they had at least three-thousand years longer to do so. Paganism is a symptom of cultural youth, Christianity a symptom of cultural mage.

Three nations: Greeks, Romans, and Jews have conquered each one in his own way, the ancient cultural world. First, the esthetic-philosophical Greeks: in Hellenism; then practical-political Romans: in the Roman empire; and ethical-religious Jews: in Christianity.

Christianity, made ethical by the Jewish Essenes (John), and intellectual by Jewish Alexandrians (Philo) was reconstructed Judaism. As far as Europe is Christian, it is (in the ethical-spiritual sense) Jewish; as far as Europe is moral, it is Jewish. Almost the whole of European ethics is rooted in Judaism. All precursors of religious or irreligious Christian morality, from Augustine to Rousseau, Kant and Tolstoy, were Jews by choice, in a spiritual way. Nietzsche is the only non-Jewish, the only pagan ethicist in Europe. The most prominent and confident representatives of Christian ideas, that in their modern rebirth are called pacifism and socialism, are Jews.

In the East, the Chinese are the ethical nation par excellence (as opposed to the esthetic-heroic Japanese and the religious-speculative Indians), in the West it is the Jews. God was head of state of the old Jews, their moral law was civil code, sin was a crime.

Judaism has remained loyal to the theocratic idea of identification of politics with ethics throughout the millennia: Christianity and socialism are both attempts to establish a Kingdom of God. Two millennia ago, the early Christians, not the Pharisees and Sadducees, inherited and revived the traditions of Moses; today it is neither the Zionists nor the Christians, but the Jewish leaders of socialism: for they also want to eradicate, with great self-denial, the original sin of capitalism, and free humanity of injustice, violence and slavery, and transform the atoned world into an earthly paradise.

To these Jewish prophets, who are preparing a new world epoch, ethics are primary in all things: politics, religion, philosophy and art. From Moses to Otto Weininger, ethics was the main issue in Jewish philosophy. In this ethical attitude toward the world lies the root of the unique greatness of the Jewish people—and at the same time the danger that Jews who lose their faith in ethics, to fall into cynical egoism: whereas others, even after loss of their ethics, still retain a wealth of knightly values and prejudices (man of honor, gentleman, cavalier, etc.) that safeguard them from a fall into value-chaos.

What separates the Jews from the average urban citizen is mainly that they are inbred people. Strength of character combined with sharp intellect predestines the most excellent specimen of the Jews to become leaders of humanity, either false or real spiritual aristocrats, and protagonists of capitalism or revolution.

PART TWO

CRISIS OF NOBILITY

1. MIND RULE INSTEAD OF SWORD RULE

Our democratic age is a miserable interlude between two great aristocratic eras: the feudal aristocracy of the sword and the social aristocracy of the mind. Feudal aristocracy is in decline, intellectual aristocracy is on the rise. The interim is called democracy, but is ruled by the pseudo-aristocracy of money.

In the Middle Ages, the rural knight ruled over the urban citizen in Europe, pagan mentality over Christian, and blood nobility over mind nobility. The knight's superiority over the citizen was based on strength of body and character, power and courage.

Two inventions conquered Middle Ages, opening the new era: the invention of gunpowder meant the end of knightly rule, and the invention of the printing press the start of intellectual rule. With the introduction of firearms, strength and courage lost their defining importance in the struggle for survival: mind, in the struggle for power and liberty, became the weapon of choice.

The printing press gave the mind power of unlimited scope: writing mankind moved into the center of a reading humanity and thus elevated the writer to intellectual leader of the masses. Gutenberg gave the feather the power that (Georg) Schwarz had taken from the sword. With the help of printing ink, Luther has conquered a greater empire than all German emperors.

In the epoch of enlightened despotism, rulers and statesmen obeyed the ideas that came from thinkers. The authors of that time formed an intellectual aristocracy of Europe. The victory of absolutism over feudalism meant the first victory of the city over the rural country, and at the same time the first stage in the victory run of mind nobility, the fall of the sword nobility. Instead of the medieval dictatorship of country over city came the modern dictatorship of city over country.

With the French revolution, which ended the privileges of the blood nobility, the second epoch of the intellectual emancipation began. Democracy is based on the optimistic premise that a nobility of mind could be recognized and elected by popular majority.

Now we are at the threshold of the third epoch of the modern age: of socialism. It, too, relies on the urban class of industrial workers, led by the aristocracy of revolutionary authors.

The influence of the blood nobility is declining, and the influence of the intellectual nobility is growing.

This development, and the chaos of modern politics, will only end when an intellectual aristocracy seizes the power resources of society: ammunition, gold and ink, and uses them for the benefit of everyone.

A decisive step towards this goal is Russian Bolshevism, where a small group of communist intellectual aristocratic rulers governs a nation and deliberately breaks with the plutocratic democracy that dominates the rest of the world today.

The struggle between capitalism and communism for the inheritance of the defeated blood nobility is a civil war between the victorious mind nobility, a war between individualism and socialism, egoism and altruism, pagan and Christian spirit. The general staff of both parties recruited from the mental ruling class of Europe: the Jews. Capitalism and communism are both rational, both mechanical, both abstract, both urban. The nobility of the sword has finally out. The effect of the mind, power of the mind, belief the in mind, and hope in the mind grows, and with it, a new nobility.

2. DAWN OF THE NOBILITY

In the course of modern times, the nobility of blood was poisoned by the courtyard atmosphere, the nobility of mind by capitalism.

Since the end of the era of knights, high nobility of continental Europe, with small exceptions, is in a state of progressive decadence. Through urbanization, it has lost its physical and mental advantage.

At the time of feudalism, blood nobility was called to protect its land against attacks by the enemy and overthrowing of their ruler. The nobleman was free and confident around subordinates, equals, and higher ranking;

like a king on his estate, his personality was able to unfold according to knightly principles.

Absolutism changed this situation: the resisting nobility, who was free, proud and brave, insisted on their historical rights, and were for the most part eradicated; the rest was pulled to the king's court and forced into resplendent servitude. This court nobility was unfree, and dependent on the whims of the ruler and his cabal; so, he lost his best attributes: character, freedom, pride, leadership. In order to break the character and thus the resistance of the French nobility, Louis XIV lured them to Versailles; the great revolution was reserved for the completion of his work: it took away the remaining rights of the nobility who had abandoned and lost their assets. Only nations in Europe retained a noble leader, where the nobility—true to their knightly mission—were the leaders and fighters of the national opposition against monarchic despotism and supremacy: England, Hungary, Poland, Italy.

Since the transformation of European culture from a knightly-rural to a civic-urban, the blood nobility fell behind ordinary citizens in intellectual terms. War, politics and the management of his estates were so demanding, that their mental abilities and interests were often stunted.

These historical causes of a new dawn of nobility were compounded by physiological ones. Instead of the hard, medieval military service, the new era brought nobility mostly unemployed life of luxury; through inherited wealth, nobility went from being the most endangered status, to the most secure; in addition, there were degenerative influences of exaggerated inbreeding, which the English nobility avoided by frequently breeding with common citizens. Through the combined effects of these circumstances, the physical, psychological and spiritual type of the aristocrat has decayed.

The intellectual nobility was not able to replace the blood nobility, because it too is in a crisis, and a state of decay. Democracy was created out of a quandary: not because people didn't want nobility, but because they couldn't find any. As soon as a new, a real nobility is constituted, democracy will disappear by itself. England, possessing real nobility, remained aristocratic, despite its democratic constitution.

Germany's academic nobility of mind, a century ago the leader of the opposition to absolutism and feudalism, and a pioneer of modern, liberal ideas, has now fallen to the mainstay of the reactionaries, the enemies of mental and political renewal. This pseudo-nobility of mind in Germany was an advocate of militarism during the war, and during the revolution a defender of capitalism. Their guiding slogans: nationalism, militarism, antisemitism, alcoholism, are also slogans in the fight against the mind. Academic intelligentsia has misjudged, denied and betrayed its responsible mission: to replace the feudal nobility and prepare a nobility of mind.

The journalistic intelligentsia has also betrayed its leadership mission. Called to become the intellectual leader and teacher of the masses, to supplement and improve what a backwards school system missed and violated, demeaned itself as the slave of capital; the tastemaker in politics and art. Its character broke under the pressure to represent and defend strangers' interests rather than its own—and its spirit became trivial by the overproduction the job demands.

Like the orator of antiquity, the journalist of the modern era stands in the center of the government machine: he moves the voters, the voters move the delegates, the delegates move the ministers. That is how the highest responsibility for every political occurrence falls on the journalist; and it's he, in typical urban spineless fashion, who feels free of any obligation and responsibility.

Schools and press are the two points from which the world could be made new and noble without bloodshed or violence. School either nourishes or poisons a child's soul; the press either nourishes or poisons the soul of an adult. Schools and press today are in the hands of an unintellectual intelligentsia: to put them back into the hands of the intellect should be the highest task of ideal politics, and ideal revolution.

The ruling dynasties of Europe have fallen through inbreeding; the dynasties of the plutocrats through a life of luxury. The nobility of blood degenerated because it became the servant of the monarchy; the nobility of mind degenerated because it became the servant of capital.

Both aristocracies had forgotten that with every privilege, every award, every exceptional position comes responsibility. They have forgotten the motto of true aristocracy: "noblesse oblige!" They chose to enjoy the fruits of their advantage without their responsibilities; they see themselves as gentlemen and superiors, not as leaders and examples to their fellow men. Instead of showing the nation new horizons, and paving the way, they let the rulers and capitalists turn them into tools for their interests: in exchange for luxury, honor and money, they sold their souls, blood and mind.

The old blood nobility as well as the mind nobility lost their claim to be called aristocracy, because they lack every sign of real aristocracy: character, freedom, responsibility. They have cut the ties they had with the nations, through social snobbery on the one hand, and educational snobbery on the other.

It is in a sense of historical nemesis that the great flood which emanates from Russia, will cleanse the world in a bloody or bloodless manner of the usurpers, who want to hold on to their privileged positions, while having long lost their mental prerequisites.

3. PLUTOCRACY

At the low point of blood—and mind nobility, it was no surprise that a third class of people temporarily seized power: the plutocrats. The form of constitution that replaced feudalism and absolutism was democracy; the form of government, plutocracy. Today, democracy is a façade of plutocracy: since nations would not tolerate a pure form of plutocracy, they were granted nominal powers, while the real power rests in the hands of plutocrats. In republican as well as monarchical democracies, the statesmen are puppets, the capitalists are the puppeteers; they dictate the guidelines of politics, rule through purchase the public opinion of the voters, and through professional and social relationships, the ministers.

Instead of the feudal structure of society, the plutocratic stepped in; birth is no more the decisive factor for social rank, but income is. Today's plutocracy is mightier than yesterday's aristocracy: because nobody is above it but the state, which is its tool and helper's helper.

When there was still true blood nobility, the system of aristocracy by birth was fairer than that of the moneyed aristocracy today: because then the ruling caste had a sense of responsibility, culture and tradition, whereas the class that rules today is barren of feelings of responsibility, culture or tradition. Rare exceptions of this don't deny this fact.

While the world view of feudalism was heroic-religious, the plutocratic society knows no higher worth than money and luxury: a person's value is estimated by what he has, not what he is.

Nevertheless, the leaders of plutocracy are building a sense of aristocracy, of selection: since a number of excellent personal characteristics are necessary to amass large wealth: drive, prudence, cleverness, level-headedness, quick-wittedness, initiative, boldness and generosity. Through these virtues the successful entrepreneurs are legitimized as modern-day conquerors whose superior will and intellectual powers are victorious over the masses of inferior competitors.

This superiority of the plutocrats only applies within their class of professionals—but it disappears when these superb money earners are compared to superb representatives of "ideal" professions. Therefor it is fair that a competent industrialist or salesman climbs higher materially and socially than his less competent colleagues—but it is not fair that he has more social power and influence than an artist, academic, politician, author, teacher, judge, or doctor, who is equally capable in his profession, but whose abilities serve "ideal" and social goals: that the current egoistical-materialistic mentality is awarded higher than the altruistic-idealistic.

The fundamental evil of a capitalistic society structure lies in the favoring of egoistical over altruistic, and materialistic over idealistic prowess; while the real aristocrats of mind and heart: the wise and kind, live in poverty and powerlessness, egoistic and violent humans usurp their positions.

Thus, plutocracy is aristocracy in its sense of energy and intellect—and pseudo-aristocracy in an ethical and spiritual sense; from a working-class view point it is aristocracy—from the view point of more ideal professions it is pseudo-aristocracy.

Just as aristocracy of blood, or of mind, so is aristocracy of wealth currently in a decaying period. The sons and grandsons of business moguls who came to great power from nothing through their will and work, slack off in luxury and idleness. Very rarely the father's drive is inherited, or is sublimated into mental or ideal creativity. The plutocratic families lack the tradition and world view, and the conservative/rural spirit that used to preserved noble families from extinction for centuries. Weak successors take over the inheritance of their fathers without themselves being gifted with the will and intellect through which it was created. Power and desire get into a conflict and undermine the internal legitimacy of capitalism. Historic progress has accelerated this natural decay. The new plutocracy of dealers that is emerging because of the economic boom of the war is displacing and replacing the plutocracy of business men. While the prosperity of the nation increases with the enrichment of business men, it decreases with enrichment of dealers. Business men are leaders of industry—dealers are parasites. Industrialism is productive, dealer syndrome is unproductive capitalism.

The current economic boom makes it easier for unscrupulous, uninhibited and irresponsible people to earn money. For speculation and dealer's profits, luck and ruthlessness are more essential than strong will and mind. The current dealer-plutocracy resembles more a kakistocracy of character than an aristocracy of great skill. Through the increasingly blurred lines between enterprise and racket, capitalism is being compromised and brought down in front of the forum of the mind and in public. No aristocracy can last without moral authority. When the ruling class stops being a symbol of ethical and esthetic values, its collapse is inevitable.

Plutocracy is, when compared to other aristocracies, poor in esthetic values. It fulfills the political functions of aristocracy, without offering any of the cultural values of nobility. But wealth is only bearable dressed in beauty, and justified only as carrier of an esthetic culture. Instead, the new plutocracy clothes itself in desolate tastelessness and brash ugliness: its wealth is barren and repulsive.

European plutocracy, unlike the American, neglects her ethical as much as her esthetic mission: social benefactors of great style are as rare as patrons. Instead of recognizing social capitalism as the purpose of their existence (to combine the fragmented national assets for generous works of a creative humanity)—the plutocrats feel justified in their oppressive majority, to irresponsibly build wealth on the backs of the miserable masses. They are exploiters of humanity, instead of trustees, misleaders instead of leaders.

Through this lack of esthetic and ethical culture, plutocracy creates hate and contempt in the public opinion and its leaders. If she doesn't empathize, she must fall.

The Russian revolution means the beginning of the end for this historical era. Despite the defeat of Lenin, his shadow will dominate the twentieth century as the French revolution, despite its fall, dominated the nineteenth: feudalists and absolutists would not have resigned voluntarily in continental Europe; they did out of fear of the terrors against the French aristocracy and king being repeated. It will be easier for the bolshevist sword of Damocles to soften the hearts of plutocrats, and make social funding available, than the gospel of Christ in two-thousand years.

4. BLOOD NOBILITY AND FUTURE NOBILITY

Nobility is defined by physical, spiritual and mental beauty; beauty of complete harmony and spiritual energy: whoever can outdo his surroundings in this way, is an aristocrat.

The old type of aristocrat is dying out; the new type has not yet been constructed, and the interim is poor in great personalities: beautiful people, noble people, and wise people. Instead, the successors of the sinking nobility usurp the dead forms of the former aristocracy and fill them with the contents of paltry bourgeois. The strong life force of the former aristocracy passed over to upstarts: but these lack its form, gentility and beauty.

Time must not despair by the idea of nobility, or the future of nobility. If humanity is to march forward, we need leaders, teachers, guides; these are examples of what humanity wishes to become; the pioneers of future elevation to higher spheres. Without nobility there is no evolution. Eudemonistic politics can be democratic—evolutionary politics must be aristocratic. To rise up and march forth, goals are necessary: reaching goals requires people: but setting and leading to these goals requires aristocrats.

The aristocrat as a leader is a political concept; the aristocrat as role model is an "ideal" concept. The highest requirement is that aristocracy coincides with nobility and leadership with role models: that perfect people become leaders.

From the majority of mankind in Europe that only believes in numbers, in majority, two quality races stand out: blood nobility and Judaism. Separate from each other, both believe in their higher calling, in their superior blood, and in the difference of the races. In these two heterogeneous superior races lies the heart of Europe's future nobility: the feudal blood nobility, as far as it is not corrupted by the court, and the Jewish nobility of mind, if it is not corrupted by money. Amongst the citizens of a better future, a few moral, high ranking rural aristocrats and a small fighting force of the revolutionary intelligence remain. The community grows into a symbol of Lenin, the man of lower rural nobility, and Trotzki, the Jewish literary figure: here the opposites of character and spirit, junker and writer, rual and urban, pagan and Christian are reconciled and a revolutionary aristocracy is created.

One small mental step forward would be enough to enlist the best elements of the blood nobility to serve this new human liberation. Their traditional courage, anti-bourgeois and anti-capitalist mentality predestines them for this position, as do their responsibility, contempt for materialistic advantage, their stoic will, integrity, and idealism. If lead onto spiritual and free paths, the strong noble energies that so far supported the reactionaries, can be regenerated and beget leader types that combine rigid will, big spirit, and selflessness; and join the ranks of the rejuvenated representatives of the nobility of mind, and to liberate and improve mankind.

In Europe, politics, for centuries was a privilege of the nobles. High nobility created an international political class where diplomatic talents were cultivated. For many generations, the European blood nobility lives in a political atmosphere from which the ordinary citizens are kept away. On their large, private estates, the aristocracy learned the art of ruling, of how to treat people—and in the leading positions of government how to treat nations. Politics is an art, not a science; it relies on instinct, not the brain. On the subconscious, not the conscious. Political talent can be awakened and nursed, not learned. Genius breaks every rule, but the nobility is richer in political talents than ordinary citizens. Because it only takes one life to acquire knowledge: but it takes many generations to acquire instincts. In science and the arts, the ordinary citizen excels the nobles: but in politics it is reverse. That is why even in democratic Europe foreign politics is delegated to the offspring of high nobility. It is in the best interest of the state to utilize for the common good the hereditary political talents which the aristocracy has absorbed for centuries. The political talents of high nobility can be traced to their strong bloodlines. This national race broadens the horizon and counteracts the bad results of inbreeding: the majority of the lower aristocrats combine the disadvantages of inbreeding, such as lack of character and spiritual poverty, whereas in the rare, high forms of nobility the positives meet: character and spirit.

Intellectually speaking, there is a gaping difference between the extreme right (conservative blood nobility) and extreme left (nobility of mind), whereas the character of those seeming opposites are very similar. But all matters intellectual, and conscious, are on the surface, and things concerning character and the unconscious lie deep in the personality. Knowledge and opinions are easier to acquire and change than character and will.

Lenin and Ludendorff are opposites in their political ideals, but brothers in their will. Had Ludendorff been raised in a revolutionary environment with Russian students, as Lenin, he would have, like Lenin, witnessed the execution of his brother by imperial hangmen. We would probably see him leading red Russia. Had Lenin been raised in a Prussian military academy, he might have become a Super-Ludendorff. What separates these two similar characters is their intellect. Lenin's dimness seems heroic and conscious, Ludendorff's seems to be naïve and unconscious. Lenin is not just a leader—he also seems spiritual; a spiritual Ludendorff so to speak.

The same parallel can be made between two other representatives of the extreme left and right: Friedrich Adler and Graf Arco. Both were murdered for idealism and martyrs for their convictions. Had Adler lived in the militaristic-reactionary environment of German blood nobility, and Arco in the socialist-revolutionary environment of Austrian aristocrats of mind, Arco's bullet would have killed prime minister Sturgkh, and Adler's bullet would have killed prime minister Eisner. Because they are brothers, separated by the difference of their instilled prejudices, and connected by their heroic, selfless characters. Here too, is the difference intellectual (Adler is spiritual) not in the purity of their thoughts. If you praise the character of one, you cannot minimize the other—as everyone does these days.

Where there is increased vitality, there is the future. The elite of the peasantry, the rural aristocrats, have (if they remained healthy) through a thousand-year symbiosis with the living and life-giving nature gathered and stored a wealth of vital forces. If new education could succeed in sublimating these enhanced life energies in the intellect, then maybe the aristocracy of the past could play a significant part in the creation of the aristocracy of the future.

5. JUDAISM AND FUTURE NOBILITY

Main bearers of corrupt as well as uncorrupt nobility of mind: capitalism, journalism, literature, are the Jews. They are predestined, through their intellectual superiority, to be a main influence on future aristocrats.

A glimpse into the history of the Jewish people will explain advantage in the battle to lead humanity. Two-thousand years ago, the Jews were a religious community comprised of ethical and spiritual individuals from all ancient nations, with their national Hebrew center in Palestine. Even then, what bound them together was primarily religion, not nation. In the course of the first thousand years, converts from all nations joined them, the last being king, nobles and citizens from Khazaria, South Russia. From then on, the religious Jewish community united as an artificial nationality and stood against all others.

Through unspeakable persecutions, Christian Europe has tried to extinguish the Jewish nation for a thousand years. The result was that Jews who were weak willed, unscrupulous, opportunistic or skeptical, were baptized, in order to escape the never-ending persecutions. Other Jews who were not clever, smart or inventive, perished under the harsh conditions.

What ultimately emerged from all these persecutions was a small community that was hardened by the heroic martyrdom for an idea, and purified of all weaknesses and poor mental qualities. Instead of destroying Judaism, Europe has against its knowledge, through artificial natural selection, raised the leading nation of the future. So, it is no wonder that this nation, the descendants of ghetto prisoners is becoming the aristocrats of the mind in Europe. Kind providence has graciously given Europe through the emancipation of the Jews a new race of aristocrats of the mind, when feudal aristocracy decayed.

The first example of this growing aristocracy of the future was the revolutionary noble Jew, Lassalle, who combined to a great extend physical beauty, character of noble courage, and sharpness of mind: aristocrat in the truest and highest sense of the word, he was a born leader and guide of his time.

Judaism is not the new nobility; but: it is the womb from which a new, intellectual nobility arises: the core around which a new intellectual nobility is grouped. An intellectual-urban "master race" is in the making: idealists, spiritual, finely tuned, just and truthful, brave as the feudal aristocrats in their best days, who happily embrace death and persecution, hate and scorn, in order to make humanity more moral, more spiritual and happier.

The Jewish heroes and martyrs of East—and Middle Europe's revolution are no less brave, enduring or idealistic than the Non-Jewish heroes of the World War—but they surpass them intellectually. The essence of those men and women who try to liberate and renew humanity is a strange synthesis of religious and political elements: heroic martyrdom, intellectual propaganda, revolutionary vigor and social love of justice and compassion. These characteristics that once made them the creators of the Christian world movement are placing them today at the top of the socialistic.

With both of these attempts at salvation (spiritual and moral) Judaism has gifted the disinherited masses of Europe more wealth than any other nation. Just as modern Judaism has more important men per capita than the other nations: barely a century after its liberation, this tiny nation is with Einstein at the top of modern science; Mahler at the top of modern music; Bergson at the top of modern philosophy; Trotsky at the top of modern politics. The prominent position that Judaism occupies today, it owes only to its superior mind, which enables it to succeed against a competition of enormously favored, hateful and envious rivals. Modern anti-Semitism is one of many reactions of the ordinary against the extraordinary; it is a modern form of ostracism of an entire nation. As a nation, Judaism experiences the eternal struggle of quantity versus quality, and inferior groups against superior individuals, as well as inferior majorities against superior minorities.

The roots of antisemitism are to be found in narrowmindedness and envy: narrowmindedness in religion or in economics; envy in intellect or economic.

Because Jews emerged from an international religious community, rather than a local race, they are the nation with the most mixed blood; because they have distanced themselves from other nations for a thousand years, are they also the nation with the most inbreeding. The chosen ones amongst them combine, like high nobility, strength of will with strength of intellect, whereas another group of Jews combine the defects of inbreeding with the defects of race mixing: a lack of character mixed with close-mindedness. Here we find the holiest of self-sacrifice next to individual selfishness, and the purest idealism next to crass materialism. Here the rule is followed: the more mixed a nation is, the less the citizens are alike, and the less possible it is to construct a single race type.

Where there is light, there are shadows. Families with geniuses show a larger percentage of mentally ill family members than average; this rule also applies to nations. Not only tomorrow's aristocrats of mind, but also today's dealer-kakistocrats recruit primarily Jews, and so sharpen the weapons of anti-Semitism.

A thousand years of slavery took from the Jews, with few exceptions, the feeling of being the master race. Constant oppression inhibits the development of the personality: it takes away the main element of the esthetic ideal of nobility. The majority of Jews suffer from this lack psychologically and physically, and it is the main reason that Europeans are instinctively against recognizing Jews as a noble race.

The resentment with which Judaism is afflicted, gives it much vital tension; but takes away noble harmony. Exaggerated inbreeding combined with hyper urbanity of their ghetto past had as a consequence trait of physical, and psychological decadence. That which the minds of the Jews gained, their bodies have lost; that which the brains of the Jews gained, their nervous systems have lost.

The Jews suffer from hypertrophy of the brain, which is the opposite of what the development of noble personality demands. The physical and nervous weakness of many intellectually superior Jews leads to a lack in physical courage (related to the highest moral courage) and insecurity in performance, traits which still are incompatible with the knightly ideal of noble men.

The intellectual master race of the Jews suffers from the characteristics of a slave race which they acquired in their historical development: there are still Jewish leaders that exhibit the posture and gestures of the oppressed slave. In their gestures, the lower aristocrats seem nobler than the most excellent Jew. These defects developed in evolution, and will disappear in evolution. Making Jews more rural (a main goal of Zionism), combined with physical education, will free the Jews from any residual of the ghetto that they still carry within. That this is possible proves the evolution of American Jews. The real freedom and power that Jews have won will soon be followed by the posture and gestures of free, powerful people.

Not only the Jews will change in the direction of the western noble ideal—but the western noble ideal will undergo a change, that will meet Judaism halfway. In a peaceful Europe of the future, nobility will take off its warlike character and replace it with an intellectual-priestly. A pacifistic and socialistic western world will not need lords and rulers—only leaders, educators and idols. In an oriental Europe, the aristocrat of the future will resemble more a Brahman and a Chinese official than a knight.

OUTLOOK

The aristocrat of the future will be neither feudal, nor Jewish, neither bourgeois nor proletarian: he will be synthetic. The races and classes of today will disappear, the personalities will remain.

Only through mixing with the best blood, the viable traits of former feudal nobility will rise to new heights; only through breeding with the top Non-Jewish Europeans will the Jewish element of the future nobility reach its full potential. To the chosen people of the future, a physically well-bred rural nobility may gift perfect bodies and gestures, and a highly educated urban nobility will add mental prowess, soulful eyes and hands.

The nobility of the past was built on quantity: feudal nobility, on the number of their ancestors; plutocracy on the number of their millions. The nobility of the future will depend on quality: on personal worth, personal perfection, perfection of the body, soul, and intellect.

Today, at the doorway of a new era, random nobility replaces hereditary nobility; instead of a noble race, noble individuals. Humans whose random blood combination elevates them to an ideal type.

From this random-nobility of today will emerge the new international and inter-social noble race of tomorrow. Everything outstanding in beauty, power, energy and intellect will recognize itself and unite according to the secret laws of *erotic attraction*. When the artificial barriers feudalism and capitalism have built fall—then the most important men will attract the most beautiful women, and the most important women will attract the most perfect men. The more perfect physically, psychologically and mentally a man is, the greater the number of women he will have to choose from. Only the noblest men will be able to choose the noblest women, and vice versa—the inferior will have to be satisfied with the inferior. The erotic life style for the inferior and the average will be "free love", for the superior: "free marriage". The race of the future nobility will not be born out of the artificial norms of human classes, but out of the divine laws of erotic eugenics.

The natural selection of human perfection will take the place of the artificial selection of feudalism and capitalism.

Socialism, which began abolishing nobility and leveling of humanity, will peak in the breeding of nobility and differentiation of humanity. Here, in social eugenics is its highest mission, which socialism does not realize, yet: to lead from unfair inequality through equality to equal inequality, over the ruins of all pseudo-aristocracy to a real, new nobility.

[illegible]

[illegible]

[illegible]

APOLOGY OF TECHNOLOGY—1922

Motto: *Ethics is the soul of our culture—technology its body: mens sana in corpore sano!*

I. THE LOST PARADISE

1 THE CURSE OF CULTURE

Culture has turned Europe into an insane asylum, and the majority of people into forced laborers. The human of the modern culture ekes out a living that is more miserable than that of an animal living in the wild. The only living beings that are even more pitiful are domestic animals, because they are even less free.

The existence of a buffalo in the jungle, a condor in the Andes, a shark in the ocean is unbelievably more beautiful, freer and happier than that of a European factory worker, who, day in and day out, hour after hour, chained to a machine, performs inorganic hand movements in order not to starve.

In prehistoric times, man was also a happy being, a happy animal. He lived in freedom, as a part of the tropical nature which fed and warmed him. His life consisted of satisfying his urges. He enjoyed life until he met a natural or a violent death. He was free, lived in nature—instead of in the state, he played—instead of work: therefor he was beautiful and happy. His courage and his joy were greater than any pain that he felt, or dangers that he faced.

Over the millennia, man lost this delicious, free existence. The Europeans, who think of themselves as the glory of civilization, live unnatural, ugly, unfree, unhealthy and lives in unnatural and ugly cities. With withered instincts and weak health, he breathes bad air in dark rooms; organized society, the state, robs him of any freedom to move or act, while the harsh climate forces him to work his entire life.

The freedom he once knew, he has lost, and with it, his luck.

2. DEVELOPMENT AND FREEDOM

With all life on earth, the end goal is development. Rocks will crystalize, plants will grow and bloom, humans and animals will live. The pleasure which only humans and animals feel, has no other value except symptomatic: animals don't satisfy their instinct because it gives them pleasure—they feel pleasure because they satisfy their instincts.

Development means growing according to internal laws: growing freedom. Any external pressure and force inhibit the freedom of development. In a deterministic world, freedom has no other meaning than dependence on inner laws, while bondage means dependence on outer conditions. The crystal does not have the freedom to choose a favorite shape; the bud does not have the freedom to grow into a favorite flower: but the freedom lies in the rock's ability to become a crystal, and that of the bud to become a flower. The unfree rock remains amorphous or crystalline—the unfree blossom withers. In both cases, the exterior force is stronger than the interior. The product of human freedom is a developed human: an unfree human is a stunted human.

If man can develop freely, he is beautiful and happy. The free, developed man is the goal of all development and the measure of all human worth.

Man has lost all freedom: this was the original sin. This is how he became an unhappy, incomplete being. All wild animals are beautiful—while most humans are ugly. There are more perfect tigers, elephants, eagles, fish, or insects than human beings, because man, through loss of his freedom, stunted and degenerate.

The prehistoric legend of the paradise lost heralds the truth that man is banished from the kingdom of freedom, of leisure, of natural living, in which the fauna of the jungle still lives today, and to which only some South Sea islanders are closest to.

This lost paradise is the time when humans lived in the tropics, like animals, because there were not yet cities, states, or work in existence.

3. OVERPOPULATION AND MIGRATION TO THE NORTH

Two things drove man out of his paradise: overpopulation and the migration into cold climates. Through overpopulation, man lost the freedom of space; everywhere, he bumps into his fellow men and their interests—and so became a slave to society.

Through migration to the north, man lost the freedom of time: his leisure. The harsh climate forces him to work against his will in order to eke out a living. So, he became a slave of northern nature.

Culture has destroyed the three forms of beauty that belonged to the natural man: freedom, leisure, nature; in their place came the state, work, and the city.

The cultured European is exiled from the South, exiled from nature.

4. SOCIETY AND CLIMATE

The two tyrants of the cultured European are named: Society and Climate.

Social bondage reaches its climax in the modern metropolis, because here overpopulation and hustle are greatest. There, people live not only next to each other, but layered on top of each another, walled in in artificial blocks of stone (houses), constantly guarded and under suspicion through the organs of society, having to submit to a number of rules and regulations, and if they don't comply, they will be tortured for years (locked up) or murdered (put to death). Social unfreedom is less severe in the country, and least severe in sparsely populated areas, as in Western United States of America, Greenland, Mongolia or Arabia. There, people can still develop in the space without getting in conflict with society; there, social freedom still exists.

The unfreedom from climate is most oppressive in the civilized nations of the North. There, man must wrest his food for the entire year from the sunless earth in a few short summer months, while at the same time protect himself from the winter frost through the procurement clothing, shelter and heat. If he resists this forced labor, he will starve or freeze to death. He is forced to tedious, exhausting work by the northern climate. He is granted more freedom in milder zones, where man must serve only one tyrant: hunger—while the other, frost, is restrained by the sun. Freest is the tropical man, because he can eat fruit and nuts without having to work. Only there exists freedom from climate.

Europe is an overpopulated, Northern strip of land; therefore, the European is the most unfree man, a slave to society and nature.

Society and nature supply each other's victims: the man who escapes the city for the country in order to leave the hustle of society, only to be threatened by the cruel climate, hunger and frost. The man who escapes the forces of nature and moves to the city in order to find safety, is threatened by a ruthless society that exploits and crushes him.

5. LIBERATION ATTEMPTS OF MANKIND

World history consists of liberation attempts of humans from the prison of society and exile of the north.

The four main ways in which humanity has tied to return to the lost paradise and leisure were these:

I. The way back (emigration): to privacy and to the sun. With this goal, people and nations have been migrating from densely populated strips of land to sparsely populated, and from colder to warmer areas. Almost all migrations of the nations, and a large number of wars can be traced back to this original yearning for freedom of movement, and for the sun.

II. The way to the top (power): out of the human hustle into seclusion, freedom and leisure of the "top ten thousand". This call sounded when due to overpopulation, power became a precondition for freedom, and due to climate conditions, power became the precondition for leisure. Only the powerful can develop without having to be considerate of his fellow man—only the powerful can escape forced labor, by making others work for him. In overpopulated nations he must choose between walking all over his fellow man or being walked on: to be lord or servant, robber or beggar. This general urge for power was the father of wars, revolutions and battles between people.

III. The way inward (ethics): away from the outward hustle into the inward seclusion, from the outward labor into the inner harmony! Liberation of man through self-control, self-constraint; sacrifice as protection from neediness, the scaling back of standards of leisure and freedom until they meet the minimum required for an overpopulated society in a harsh climate. All religious movements can be traced back to this urge: to substitute the outer unfreedom and labor with the calmness of the heart.

IV. The way forward (technology): out of the era of slave labor into a new era of freedom and leisure through the victory of the human spirit over the forces of nature! The overcoming of overpopulation through increase in productivity and of slave labor through the enslavement of the forces of nature. Technological and scientific progress is based on this urge to break the tyranny of nature.

II. ETHICS AND TECHNOLOGY

1. THE SOCIAL QUESTION

The question about the destiny of European culture is: "How will it be possible to protect mankind living on a narrow, cold and barren strip of land from famine, hypothermia, homicide and exhaustion, and give to it the freedom and leisure that once gave it happiness and beauty?"

The answer is: "Through the development of ethics and technology." Ethics in schools, the press and in religion can transform European man from predator into a domestic animal, and make him mature enough for a free society. Technology can give the European free time and energy through increased productivity and through operating machines instead of hard labor, which is needed to expand culture.

Ethics solves the social problem from within, technology from without—in Europe, only two classes of people have the prerequisites for happiness: the rich, because they can do and have whatever they want, and the holy, because they don't want to do or have more than their destiny grants them. The rich conquer an objective freedom through the power they have to turn their fellow men and the forces of nature into a tool for their will—and the holy conquer a subjective freedom, through their indifference with which they view earthly goods. The rich can develop outwardly—the holy inwardly.

All remaining Europeans are slaves of nature and society: forced laborers and prisoners.

2. INADEQUACY OF POLITICS

It is the ideal of ethics to create a society of saints in Europe; it is the ideal of technology to create a society of wealthy Europeans. Ethics wants to abolish greed, so that people don't *feel* poor—technology wants to abolish hardship, so that people don't have to *be* poor.

Politics is not in a position to make people happy or rich. That is why their arbitrary attempts to answer the social question must fail. Only in the service of ethics or technology can politics participate in the solution of the social question.

With the current state of ethics and technology, politics would only be able to universalize unfreedom, poverty and forced labor. It could only equalize the evil, not cancel it. It could turn Europe into a penitentiary of equal slaves—but not a paradise. The citizen of the ideal social state today would be less free and more tormented than South See islanders in their natural state. Cultural history would be the history of a disastrous fraud on humanity.

3. STATE AND EMPLOYMENT

As long as ethics are too insignificant to protect human beings from each other, and technology not developed enough to shift the workload on to the forces of nature, humanity will try to ward off the damages of overpopulation through the state, the damages of the climate through work.

The state protects humans from arbitrariness of other humans—work protects him from the forces of nature.

The organized, "coercive state" grants, under certain conditions, protection from murder and robbery of citizens who are willing to give up their freedom, and organized forced labor grants protection from hunger and frost to those willing to give up their energy and time.

These two institutions pardon the Europeans, who naturally would be doomed to die, to lifelong forced labor. To save their lives, they must give up their freedom. As a citizen of the state he is locked into the cage of his rights and obligations—as forced laborer in the hard yoke of his performance. If he rejects the state, he faces the gallows; if he rejects labor, he faces starvation.

4. ANARCHY AND LEISURE

Both the state and labor pretend to be *ideals*—demanding awe and love from their victims. But they are not ideals—they are social and climatic necessities which are unbearable.

Since the states came into existence, humanity dreams of anarchy, the ideal condition that is free of the state, and since labor came into existence, humans dream of leisure, the ideal condition of free time.

Anarchy and leisure are ideals—not state and labor.

Anarchy is not possible in a densely populated society which does not have high ethical standards. Its realization would have to destroy the remaining freedom and chance of survival of the citizens. In the general panic of colliding egos, people would oppress each other. Anarchy would lead to total unfreedom.

Universal leisure would lead to the death by starvation or hypothermia of the majority of people in the north. Distress and misery would reach their peak.

Insulated anarchy exists in the deserts of Bedouins, and in the snow fields of Eskimos. Leisure exists in thinly populated and fertile southern nations.

5. OVERCOMING OF STATE AND LABOR

The coercive state and forced labor, the protectors and tyrants of civilization, cannot be overcome by a political revolution, but only by ethics and technology. Until ethics overcomes the coercive state, anarchy means universal murder and theft; until technology overcomes forced labor, leisure can only mean universal starvation and hypothermia.

Only through ethics can citizens of overpopulated nations escape the tyranny of society, and through technology the citizens in cold climates can escape the tyranny of the forces of nature.

Mission of the state is to make itself unnecessary through ethics, and finally lead to anarchy. Mission of labor is to make itself unnecessary through technology, and finally lead to leisure.

The voluntary human society is not a curse—only the forced state. Voluntary labor is not a curse—only forced labor. Not wantonness is ideal, but freedom; not laziness, but leisure.

The coercive state and forced labor are things that must be overcome: but they cannot be overcome by anarchy and leisure before ethics and technology are complete; to achieve this, humans must develop the coercive state to develop ethics, and develop forced labor to develop technology.

The road to an ethical anarchy leads through a forced state, and leads to technical leisure through forced labor.

The curves of the cultural spiral that leads from the paradise of the past to the paradise of the future, run as follows:

Natural anarchy—overpopulation—coercive state—ethics—cultural anarchy.

And natural leisure—emigration to the north—forced labor—technology—cultural leisure.

We are currently in the center of these curves, equally far from both past and future paradise: that is the reason for our misery. The average modern European is no longer a natural human being—but not yet civilized; no longer animal—but not yet human; no longer part of nature—but not yet ruler of nature.

6. ETHICS AND TECHNOLOGY

Ethics and technology are sisters: Ethics rule the natural energy within us—technology rules the natural forces around us. Both seek to conquer nature through formative spirit.

Ethics seek to redeem humanity through heroic denial—technology through heroic affirmation (action).

Ethics turn the will to power inward: it wants to conquer the microcosm. Technology turns the will to power outward: it wants to conquer the macrocosm. Neither ethics nor technology alone can save the northern man, because a starving and freezing man cannot be sated and warmed through ethics, and a wicked and covetous mankind cannot be protected from itself.

What good are morals if humanity starves and freezes? What good is technological progress if humans misuse it to slaughter and maim one another?

Civilized Asia suffers from overpopulation more than from hypothermia. It could, therefor, forgo technology much easier than Europe, where ethics and technology must complement each other.

III. ASIA AND EUROPE

1. ASIA AND EUROPE

Asia's greatness lies in its ethics—Europe's greatness in its technology. Asia is a teacher/master of self-control for the world. Europe is the teacher/master in the mastery over nature. In Asia, the main focus of the social question is in overpopulation—in Europe it is in climate.

Asia must enable peaceful cohabitation of the majority of people: it can accomplish this through educating its citizens in ethics (selflessness and self-control).

Europe must exorcise the horrors of starvation and hypothermia which constantly threaten her citizens. She can achieve this only through technology (work and invention). There are two core values in life: harmony and energy—on which all other values are dependent.

Asia's greatness and beauty depends on harmony.

Europe's greatness and beauty depends on energy. Asia lives in the dimension of space: its spirit is tranquil, inward-looking, calm; it is feminine, plant-like, static, Apollonian, classic, idyllic. Europe lives in the dimension of time: its spirit is active, directed outwards, moving and determined; it is masculine, animalistic, dynamic, Dionysian, romantic, heroic.

Asia's symbol is the all-encompassing sea, the circle—Europe's symbol is the forward-looking power, the straight line. Here, the deepest meaning of the cosmic symbols, the

Alpha and Omega, is revealed. It conveys to us the mystical, recurrent polarity, of force and form, time and space, man and cosmos, that hides behind the souls of Europe and Asia; the capital Omega, the circle, that opens the gate to the cosmos, is a symbol of the divine harmony of Asia; the capital Alpha, a sharp upwards-pointing arrow that pierces through the circle, is a symbol of the action and determination Europe's which breaks the eternal calmness of Asia. A and O are also in the Freudian sense unmistakable symbols of masculinity and femininity: the union of these symbols signifies conception and life, as well as reveals the eternal dualism of the world. The same symbolism probably exists in the numbers 1 and 0, as the finite 1 against the infinite 0 — "yes" against "no".

2. CULTURE AND CLIMATE

The souls of Asia and Europe emerged out of the Asian and European climates. Asia's cultural centers are located in warm—Europe's cultural centers in cold areas. This reveals their opposing relationships to nature: while a Southerner feels like a child and a friend of nature, in the North one is forced to wrest everything he needs to live, in a hard battle against the cold earth. He has two choices: being the master, or the slave of nature—and definitely an opponent.

In the South, the confrontation between man and nature was friendly, harmonious. In the North, warlike and heroic.

Europe's dynamic explains itself because it is the cultural center of the world. For tens of thousands of years, cold and lack present Europeans with a choice: "Work or die!" If one couldn't work, he had to starve to death or die of hypothermia. For many generations, the winter has systematically eradicated weak, passive, sluggish, inward-looking Europeans, and bred a hard, energetic and heroic human race.

Since prehistoric times, the white race—even longer the whites with blond hair—wrestle with winter, which made them paler and paler, but also tougher and tougher. It is this hardening that Europeans owe their superior health and energy until this day.

The white man is the son of winter, the lack of sunshine: To overcome this, he had to use muscle and mind to the fullest to create “new suns”; he had to battle an eternally unfriendly nature, and to conquer it.

The choice between action and death created in the North of every culture its strongest, most heroic type: in Europe it is the German, in Asia it is the Japanese, in America, the Aztek. Heat forces man to limit his activity to a minimum, the cold forces him to increase it to a maximum.

The active, heroic man of the North has always conquered the more passive, harmonious South; for that, the cultured South assimilated and civilized the barbaric northerners—until he was conquered, barbarized and regenerated by a new North.

Most military conquests in history are started by northern states against the South, and most spiritual-religious conflicts started by southern states against the North.

Europe was conquered in a religious war by the Jews, and militaristically by Germans. In Asia, the religions of

India and Arabia won, while it is politically dominated by Japan.

The more active nations of warmer areas (Arabs, Turks, Tartars, Mongolians) originated in deserts or steppes. There, instead of the cold, the drought was their disciplinarian; but here also, inevitably, victory of the heroic man over the idyllic took place; victory of the active over the passive, and the hungry over the well-fed.

3. THE THREE RELIGIONS

India's heat, that paralyzes every activity, created their contemplative mentality; Europe's cold, which forces human activity, created an active mentality; Chinas temperate climate, which encourages a harmonious rotation between activity and tranquility, created a harmonious mentality.

The three different climates created three different types of religions: the contemplative, the heroic and the harmonious.

The heroic religion and ethics of the North is expressed in Edda as well as in the world view of European and Japanese knighthood, experiencing its resurrection in the teachings of Nietzsche. Its highest virtue and energy are the battle and the hero: Siegfried. The contemplative religions and ethics of the South find perfection in Buddhism. Its highest virtue is self-restraint and gentleness, its highest ideal is peace and the Buddha.

The harmonious religion and ethics of the middle unfolded in Greece in the West, and in China in the East. It required neither asceticism of battle, nor self-restraint. It is optimistic and worldly; Its ideal is the noble man: wise Confucius, the artist Apollo. The Greek ideal of the Apollonian man stands in the middle, in between the German hero Siegfried, and the Indian holy one, Buddha.

All religious organizations are combinations of these three basic types. Every religion that spreads out, must adjust to these climatic conditions. Asian Christians of the south, Catholics of the middle, and Protestants of the North are similar. The same applies to Buddhists in Ceylon, China and Japan. Christianity has transmitted the Asian values of the South into our culture. Renaissance has given us the old values of the middle; knighthood has transmitted the German values of the North.

4. HARMONY AND FORCE

Europe's cultural values are mixed—its spirit is predominantly Nordic.

Asians are superior to Europeans in kindness and wisdom, bur trail Europeans in energy and cleverness.

European "honor" is a heroic value—the Asian "dignity" is a harmonic value. Constant battle hardens, constant peace softens the heart. Therefor the Asian is milder and gentler than the European. Additionally, Indian, Chinese, Japanese and Jewish society is much older than that of Germans, who until 2000 years ago lived in anarchy. Asians have developed their social virtues better and longer than Europeans.

The goodness of the heart corresponds to the wisdom of the mind. Wisdom is based on harmony—intelligence is based on sharpness of the mind.

Wisdom is a fruit of the more mature South, but rarely exists in the North. Even the European philosophers are rarely wise, the ethicists rarely kind. Ancient culture was richer in wise men, whose personalities were marked by spirituality, whereas they are almost extinct in modern Europe (under Christianity). The reason is the relatively young German culture, and the vehemence of the German spirit. Also, the monasteries were the only sanctuaries for contemplative wisdom in the middle ages. The wise men retreated and died there, as victims of their chastity vows.

European depictions of Christ are serious and sad, while Buddha's statues smile. European thinkers are deeply serious—whereas the wise in Asia smile, because they live in harmony with themselves, their society and with nature—not in battle; they try every reform on themselves, instead of others, and have an effect on others through their example, rather than books. Beyond thinking, they rediscover their childhood—while Europe's thinkers age too early.

Nevertheless, Europe is as great as Asia, but her greatness does not lie in her goodness or her wisdom—but in her productivity and innovation.

Europe is the hero of the world; on every battle front of humanity, it is at the top: in hunting, war and technology, Europeans have accomplished more than any other culture in history. They have almost eradicated all dangerous animals; conquered almost all dark-skinned nations, as well as, through science and technology achieved such total domination over nature as never has been thought possible. Asia's world mission is the salvation of humanity through ethics—Europe's world mission is to liberate humanity through technology.

Europe's symbol is not the wise, the saint, the martyr—but the hero, the fighter, the winner, the liberator.

IV. EUROPE'S TECHNOLOGICAL WORLD MISSION

1. THE EUROPEAN SPIRIT

With the modern age begins the cultural mission Europe's. The essence of Europe is the will to change and improve the world through action. Europe consciously strives from the present into the future; it is in a constant state of emancipation, reformation, revolution; it is addicted to renewal, skeptical, impious, and wrestles with its customs and traditions.

In Jewish mythology, the European spirit corresponds to Lucifer—in the Greek, Prometheus: the light-bringer who carries the divine spark to earth, and who rebels against the heavenly-Asian harmony, the divine world order; the prince of the world, the father of battle, of technology, of enlightenment and of progress; the leader of man in his struggle against nature.

The spirit of Europe has broken political despotism and the domination of the forces of nature. The European does not yield to his fate, but seeks to master it through his actions and mind, as an activist and a rationalist.

2. GREECE AS PRE-EUROPE

Greece was the precursor of Europe; it first perceived the essential difference between itself and Asia, and discovered its activist-rationalist soul. Its Olympus was not the paradise of peace, but a site of battles; its highest god was an impious rebel. Greece overthrew kings and gods, and put in their place the state of the citizen and the religion of man.

This European period of Greece began with the fall of the tyrants and ended with the "Asian" despotism of Alexander and his successors; it was briefly continued in the republic of Rome and ended for good with the Roman Empire.

Alexander the Great, Greek kings and Roman emperors were the heirs of the Asian idea of great kingdoms. The Roman empire was no different from the despotic regimes in China, Mesopotamia, India and Persia.

In the middle ages, Europe was a cultural suburb of Asia. It was ruled by the Asian religion of Jesus. European religious culture, mystic mood, monarchical form of government and the dualism of popes and emperors, of monks and knights—these were all Asian.

Europe came to its senses through the emancipation from Christianity that started with the renaissance and reformation, and continued with Nietzsche, and spiritually separated from Asia.

3. THE TECHNICAL BASICS OF EUROPE

The world of Philipp II did not significantly alter our world culture since the Hammurabi. Neither in art, nor science, not politics, judiciary or administration. The world has changed more dramatically in the last 350 years than in the 3500 years prior.

It was technology that awoke Europe from her Sleeping Beauty slumber of the middle ages. Technology defeated knighthood and feudalism through the invention of firearms, and popedom and superstition through the invention of the printing press; through the compass and ship technology foreign parts of the world opened up, and were conquered with the help of gunpowder.

The progress of modern science is inseparable from technology. Without a telescope, there would be no modern astronomy, without a microscope there would not be bacteriology. Even modern art is related to technology. Modern instrumental music, modern architecture and modern theater are based partially on technology. The impact that photography has on portrait painting will increase. Since photography is unsurpassed in the reproduction of the facial form, painters will be forced to look inward and capture the abstract nature and soul of man. A similar effect as photography has on painting could also apply to cinematography and theater.

Modern strategy has fundamentally changed under the influence of technology. Warfare has changed from a psychological to a technological science. Today's methods of war methods differ more significantly from those of the middle ages than these differ from the combat of primitive people.

All of today's politics point to a technological progress: democracy, nationalism and national education are based on the invention of the printing press. Industrialism and colonial imperialism, capitalism and socialism are consequences of technological progress and a changing global economy. Just as agriculture once created a patriarchal, and crafts once created an individualistic mentality—so will collective, organized industrialism create a socialist mentality. Organization of labor through technology creates a socialist organization of workers.

At last, progress in technology has changed the European. He is more rushed and nervous, less settled, more awake, alert, rational, active, practical, and smarter.

If we delete all the consequences technology had on our culture, that which remains is in no way more evolved than ancient Egyptian or Babylonian culture—in some respect it is less evolved.

Europe owes its cultural advantage to technology. Only through technology has Europe become the master and leader of the world.

Europe is a function of technology—America is an escalation of Europe.

4. TECHNOLOGICAL WORLD CHANGE

The age of technology in Europe is a phenomenon in world history that can be compared to the invention of heating in primeval times. The invention of fire sparked the history of human culture and the domestication of the human animal. All subsequent mental and material progress of humanity are based on this discovery by primeval Prometheus.

Technology marks a similar turning point in human history as fire does. In ten thousand years history will be divided in the pre- and post-technological ages. **The Europeans—who, by that time will be long extinct**—will, as the fathers of the technological world change, be praised as saviors.

The possible effects of a technological age which we are now entering are unmistakable. Technology is creating the foundations of all cultures which, because of the changed conditions will differ from any current cultures.

All cultures to date, from ancient Egypt to the middle ages have become progressively more similar because they were based on certain technical principals. There was no significant technological progress from the ancient Egyptians to the end of the middle ages.

The culture that will emerge from the technological age will differ as much from the ancient and middle ages as those differed from the stone ages.

5. EUROPE AS CULTURAL AGENT

Europe is a cycle of culture—a cultural tangent: the tangents that developed from the cycle of Asian culture have bloomed, wilted and risen again in another location.

Europe blew up this cycle and instead introduced a direction of unknown life forms.

Everything already existed in the Oriental cultures of the East and West: the technological culture Europe's is truly an unknown, truly something new.

Europe is a bridge between the complex, known cultures throughout history and the cultural forms of the future.

One era that compares to the European in meaning and dynamics, but whose traces are lost, must have preceded the ancient Babylonian culture, the ancient Chinese and Egyptian culture. This Pre-Europe created the foundation for all the cultures of the last millennia; like modern Europe, it was a cultural tangent that separated from the cycle of the ancient precultures.

The sequence of the great world history consists of Asian cycles and European cultural tangents. Without these tangents (which are only European in a spiritual, not a geographical sense) there would only be expansion, not development. After a long period of maturity, one ingenious nation emerges from the darkness, blows up the natural course of culture and raises humanity to a higher level.

Inventions, not poetry or religion mark these states of cultural developments: the invention of bronze, iron, electricity. These inventions build the eternal legacy of an era for all future cultures. Nothing will remain from the ancients—while the modern era is enriching culture through the conquest of electricity and other natural forces: these inventions will survive Faust, the Divine Comedy, and the Iliad.

With the middle ages, the cultural cycle of iron ended—with the modern age, the cultural cycle of the machine is beginning; not a new culture, but a new era.

Creators of this technological era is the ingenious Promethean nation of "Germanized" Europeans. Modern culture is founded as much on their innovative spirit as on the ethics of the Jews, the art of the Greeks, and the politics of the Romans.

6. LEONARDO AND BACON

At the start of the age of technology, two great Europeans have sensed the meaning of Europe: Leonardo da Vinci and Bacon von Verulam. Leonardo dedicated himself to technology with as much passion as to art. His favorite problem was human flight, the solution of which our era has witnessed.

It is said that there are yogis in India who can, through ethics and asceticism, break the laws of gravity and float in the air. In Europe, the inventive spirit of engineers and their materialization: the airplane conquered the laws of gravity through technology. Levitation and aviation symbolically represent the Asian and European forms of human power and freedom.

Bacon was the creator of the bold utopian novel "New Atlantis". Its technological character distinguishes it from all previous utopias, from Plato to Thomas Morus. The shift from middle-age/Asian thinking to modern-age/European is found in the contrast between Morus' ethical/political "Utopia" and Bacon's "New Atlantis". Morus still sees social-ethical reforms as the lever of world improvement, Bacon the technological inventions.

Morus was still a Christian—Bacon was European.

V. HUNTING—WAR—WORK

1. POWER AND FREEDOM

The contemplative man lives in peace with his surroundings, the active man in a constant state of war. For self-preservation, fulfillment and development, he must constantly fight foreign powers, destroy and enslave.

The fight for survival is a fight for freedom and power. Victory means: to enforce his will. Only the winner is free, mighty. There is no line between freedom and power: the full enjoyment of one's freedom hurts foreign interests. Power is the only assurance of uninhibited freedom.

Humanity's fight for freedom coincides with the fight for power. In its course humanity has conquered the globe: the animal kingdom through hunting and breeding—the plant kingdom through agriculture—the mineral kingdom through mining—natural forces through technology. From a nondescript, weak animal, man rose up as the lord of the world.

2. HUNTING

The first phase of human struggle was the age of hunting.

After hundreds of thousands of years of battles, man has won domination over the animal world. This victorious fight of relatively weak man against all extinct and still existing large and wild animal species is a greatness that can be compared to the conquest of the ancient world by a small village, Rome.

Man won against all horns and teeth, paws and claws of his better equipped rival only with the weapon of his superior mind, which he continually sharpened in the fight.

The goals in the human war against his animal enemies were defensive and offensive: protection and enslavement.

At first, man was content to render his enemies harmless through defense and extermination; later, he began to tame and use them. He turned wolves into dogs, buffalo into cattle, wild elephants, camels, donkeys, horses, lamas, goats, sheep and cats into domestic ones. He subdued a host of former rivals into an army of animal slaves, an arsenal of living machines, to work and fight for him, and to increase his freedom and his power.

3. WAR

To maintain the power he won, and to increase it, man moved to fight his fellow man with the same methods as he fought the animal kingdom. The era of hunting became the era of war. Man fought with man over the distribution of the conquered earth. The stronger warded off the weaker, and either killed or enslaved him: war was a special form of hunting, slavery a special form of animal husbandry. In the fight for freedom and power, the stronger, bolder and wiser won over the weaker, the cowardly, and dumber. War also sharpened the human mind and manpower.

4. WORK

In the long run, hunting and war could not feed humanity. Changing again, man went to war against inanimate nature. The age of work began. Wars and hunting still brought fame and glory—but the emphasis of life shifted towards work, because it gave him food, which he needed for his preservation.

Work was a special form of war—technology a special form of slavery: instead of humans, natural forces were dominated and enslaved.

Through work man fought hunger: he subdued the ground and the crops and reaped the profit. Through work, man fought against the winter. He built houses, wove fabrics, felled wood. He protected himself against the forces of nature through work.

5. WAR AS ANACHRONISM

The way hunting, war and work merged into each other, makes it impossible to separate them chronologically. For thousands of years, the age of hunting ran parallel to the age of war, as today the age of war runs parallel to the age of work; but the center of gravity of war shifted and shifts continually. While originally hunting was at the center of human activity, war took its place, and finally, work.

War, which was once necessary for the advancement of culture, lost its meaning and has become a dangerous destroyer of culture. Today it is inventions that mark progress, not wars.

Today, humanity's deciding battles for freedom play out in work.

In time, when the world war will fascinate only historians, our turn of the century will be famous for the birth of aviation.

In the era of war, hunting acted as anachronism, so in the era of work, war acts as anachronism. But in this era, every war is a civil war because it is directed toward fellow fighters and the entire army of workers.

In the era of work, the glorification of war is as untimely as the glorification of hunting in the era of war. Originally, the dragon and lion slayer were heroes; then it was the commander; finally, it is the inventor. Lavoisier has contributed more to the human development than Robespierre and Bonaparte put together.

As the hunter ruled the era of hunting, the warrior in the era of war, the worker will rule in the era of work.

6. TECHNOLOGY

The era of work is divided into agriculture and technology.

As a farmer, man is defensive against nature—as technician he is offensive.

The methods of work correspond to those of war and hunting: defense and enslavement. The era of agriculture is limited to ward off hunger and cold, while technology goes beyond, to enslave once harmful natural forces. Man rules over steam and electricity, and over a slave army of machines. With these he not only defends himself against hunger and cold, natural disaster and diseases, but he even tries to tackle the barriers of time, space and gravity. His battle for freedom from the forces of nature crosses into a struggle for power over such forces.

Technology is the practical application of science for the domination of nature. Chemistry, as in atomic engineering and medicine, is in a sense organic technology.

Technology intellectualizes work; it lessens the work load and increases profit.

Technology is founded on a heroic and activist attitude towards nature; it does not obey the will of nature, but dominates it. The will to power is the motivating force for progress. The technician sees a tyrant in the forces of nature, that must be overthrown—an enemy that must be defeated. Technology is the child of the European spirit.

VI. TECHNOLOGY'S CAMPAIGN

1. EUROPE'S MASS MISERY

Through the population increase, the situation is becoming increasingly desperate for the European. Despite all previous advances in technology, he is still in a miserable state. He has pushed back the ghosts of famine and hypothermia—at the price of his freedom and leisure.

For the European, fruitful forced labor begins at age seven with forced schooling, and ends, usually, with death. His childhood is poisoned by his preparation for a life of fighting, which in the following decades devours his time, personality, vitality and zest for life. Leisure is punished by the death penalty. The average, asset-less European citizen has two choices: either work to exhaustion, or starve to death, together with his children. The whip of hunger drives him to continue to work, despite exhaustion, disgust and bitterness.

The European nations have made two political attempts at improving this wretched state: colonial policy and socialism.

2. COLONIAL POLICY

The first form of colonial policy consists of conquest and settlement in thinly populated areas of land by nations suffering from overpopulation. Emigration is actually able to save nations from overpopulation, and secure a dignified existence for people who find the European hustle unbearable. Emigration still offers millions of people an escape from European hell, and should therefor be promoted in every way.

The second form of colonial policy consists of exploitation of warmer areas and colored peoples. People of southern races are roused from their golden leisure with European cannons and rifles, and forced to work in the service of Europe. The poorer, but stronger North systematically plunders the richer but weaker South; it steals the wealth, freedom, and leisure, and uses them for its own wealth, freedom and leisure.

Several European nations have this robbery and slavery to thank for their prosperity, which enables them to improve the lives of their own workers.

It will fail in the long run: because the inevitable outcome will be an enormous revolt of slaves, and Europeans will be expelled from the colored colonies and Europe's tropical culture base will be overthrown.

Even emigration is only a provisional solution. Some colonies are now almost as overpopulated as their motherlands, approaching a similar misery. The time must come when there are no more deserted areas on earth.

By then, new ways have to be found to counter the European doom.

3. SOCIAL POLICY

The second effort to alleviate European mass misery is socialism.

Socialism will exorcise the European hell through even distribution of the workload and earnings. There is no doubt the fate of the masses could be much improved through sensible reforms. But if social progress is not supported by a boom in technology, the misery can only be alleviated, not eliminated.

The workload that is necessary to feed and provide warmth for too many Europeans is huge; the earnings from a rough and not fertile enough Europe is relatively small; even equal distribution would result in too much work, and too little pay for every European. At today's level of technology, life in a socialist Europe would dissolve in a double activity: work to eat, and eat to work. The equality ideal would be realized, but Europe would be further removed from freedom, leisure and culture than ever before. To liberate humanity, Europe is too barbaric, and too poor. The fortune of the few wealthy, if equally distributed to all, would disappear; poverty would not be eliminated, but generalized.

Socialism alone is not able to lead Europe out of misery and bondage into liberty and prosperity. Neither ballots, nor stocks can compensate a coal miner for a life spent in mines and shafts. Most slaves of Asian despots are freer than the "free" worker of socialized labor.

Socialism is misjudging the "European Problem" when it sees unfair distribution as the problem for the European economy—not insufficient production. The roots of the European misery lie in the need for forced labor, not in unfair distribution. Socialism mistakenly sees capitalism as root cause for fruitful forced labor under which Europe is suffering; in reality, only a small percentage of the labor output flows to the capitalists and their luxuries; the largest part of the labor serves to turn a barren area of the world fertile, and a cold into a warm, to sustain the number of humans which would naturally all perish.

Winter and overpopulation in Europe are harder and crueler despots than all the capitalists. Nevertheless, politicians are not leading the European revolution against these ruthless tyrants—but inventors.

4. TECHNOLOGICAL WORLD REVOLUTION

Colonial Imperialism, like Socialism, are painkillers, not cures, for the European disease; they can alleviate the pain, not heal the disease; put off the catastrophe, but not prevent it. Europe will have to decide to either decimate its population and commit suicide—or to recover through greatly increasing production and perfecting technology.

Europe must understand that technological progress is a liberation war against the hardest, cruelest and most uncharitable tyrant: Nordic nature.

It depends on the result of this revolution whether humanity uses the once-in-eons opportunity to become the master of nature—or whether it is a wasted opportunity, perhaps forever.

One-hundred years ago, Europe opened the offensive against the superior nature, against which, up to that point, it had only defended itself. Europe was no longer satisfied being at the mercy of the natural forces, but began to enslave its enemies.

Technology has begun supplementing the army of slave animals, and replacing the army of slave workers through machines which are operated by natural forces.

5. TECHNOLOGY'S ARMY

Europe (as well as America) has mobilized the globe for the greatest and most momentous war.

The frontline soldiers of the global army of laborers fighting against the will of the natural forces are the industrial workers; their officers are engineers, entrepreneurs and managers; inventors are the General Staff; the machines are the Artillery; the mines are their trenches; factories are the forts.

With this army, and the reserves he draws from all parts of the world, the white man hopes to break the tyranny of mother nature, and subdue her forces to the human spirit, and finally liberate man.

6. THE ELECTRIC WAR

Technology's army has won its first decisive victory over one of mankind's oldest antagonists: lightning.

Since time immemorial, the electric spark as lightning has threatened, wounded, and killed man; it burned his homes and slain his cattle. For thousands of years man was exposed to this treacherous enemy who never helped him in any way, until Benjamin Franklin broke its rule of terror by inventing the lightning rod. The electric spark as the scourge of mankind was thus warded off. But the *white man* was not satisfied with this defensive victory; he went on the offensive and, in one century, managed to turn this enemy into a slave, turning this most dangerous predator into a useful pet.

Today the electric spark that once filled our forefathers with horror lights our rooms, cooks our tea, irons our laundry, rings our bells, carries our letters (telegrams), pulls trains and wagons, drives machines—in a word, became our messenger, postman, servant, cook, heater, lighting, worker, carrier and even our hangman. What the electric spark in Europe and America does today in the service of mankind would not be possible, even if human working hours were doubled.

Just as this formerly hostile natural force was not only beaten back, but was transformed into the indispensable and most useful servant of man, so too will the floods of the sea, the heat of the sun, storms and floods one day become the slaves of men. Poisons become remedies, deadly viruses become vaccinations. Just as man used to tame and subdue wild animals in primeval times, modern man is taming and subjugating the wild forces of nature.

By such victory, Nordic man will one day conquer freedom, leisure and culture. Not through depopulation or renunciation, not through war and revolution—but through invention and work, through spirit and action.

7. THE INVENTOR AS REDEEMER

In our European epoch, the inventor is a greater benefactor of humanity than the saint.

The inventor of the automobile has done more for horses and spared them more suffering than any animal welfare association in the world. The car is about to save thousands of East Asian rickshaw operators from a life as a draft animal.

The inventors of diphtheria and its antitoxins have saved the lives of more children than all baby hospitals.

The galley-slaves owe their liberation to modern ship technology, while with the introduction of petroleum heating modern technology is beginning to liberate the ship's fire stokers from their hellish profession.

The inventor who, by atomic destruction, finds a practical substitute for coal will have done more for mankind than the most successful reformer, because he will rescue millions of coal workers from their inhumane existence and wipe out a large part of the human workload, whereas today no communist dictator could avoid condemning people to that life underground.

The chemist who succeeds in making wood edible, would free the people from the yoke of famine, which has been suppressing them longer and more cruelly than any human domination.

Neither ethics, nor art, nor religion, nor politics will wipe out the biblical curse, but technology. Organic technology—medicine, is expected to banish the woman's curse: "With painful labor you will give birth to children." Inorganic technology is expected to banish the man's curse: "By the sweat of your brow you will eat your bread."

In many respects, our age is similar to the beginning of the Roman empire. At that time, the world hoped for salvation through the empire's *Pax Romana*. The hoped-for change came, but from a completely different direction. Not from the outside, but from within. Not by politics, but religion. Not by Caesar Augustus, but Jesus Christ.

We too are facing a world turn. Humanity today expects the socialist era to be the dawn of the golden era. The hoped-for world change will come, maybe, but not through politics, but by technology. Not by a revolutionary, but by an inventor. Not through Lenin, but by a man who may already be living nameless somewhere today and who will someday succeed in liberating humanity from famine, frost and forced labor by opening up new, unimagined energy sources.

VII. ENDGOAL OF TECHNOLOGY

1. CULTURE AND SLAVERY

Every previous culture was based on slavery: the ancient on slaves, the medieval on serfs, the modern on the working class. The importance of the slaves is based on the fact that they create freedom and leisure (preconditions for any culture) for their lords through their own lack of freedom and excessive working. Because it is not possible for the same people to perform the monstrous physical labor necessary for food, clothing and housing of a generation, and at the same time perform the mental work necessary for the creation and maintenance of a culture.

Everywhere there exists a division of labor: so that the brain can think, the stomach must digest; without rooting its roots in the earth, no plant can flower. The bearers of every culture are developed people. Development is impossible without the atmosphere of freedom and leisure; even rocks can only crystallize in a liquid, free state. Where it is enclosed, unfree, it must remain amorphous.

The culture-building freedom and leisure of the few could only be created through bondage and excessive laboring of the many. In northern and overpopulated parts of the world, the divine existence of thousands was always and everywhere built on one-hundred thousand living like animals.

The modern age, with its Christian, social ideas, stood before two choices: either to renounce culture or to maintain slavery. Aesthetic considerations were against the first choice—ethical considerations against the second. The first was resisted by taste, the second by emotion.

Western Europe opted for the second choice. In order to preserve the rest of its bourgeois culture, slavery remained, but disguised in industrial labor—while Russia is preparing to make the first choice, liberating the labor force, but sacrificing its entire culture for this liberation of the slaves.

Both solutions are unbearable. The human spirit must look for an escape from this dilemma; it is found in technology. Technology alone can break slavery and save culture.

2. THE MACHINE

The ultimate goal of technology is the replacement of slave labor through machine-work: elevating the whole of humanity into a class of men, in whose service an army of natural forces works in the form of machines.

We are on the way to this goal. In the past, almost all technical energies had to be generated by human or animal muscles. Today, they are frequently replaced by steam, electricity and motorization. More and more, people are assuming the role of a manager of energy, instead of a generator. Even yesterday, the worker pulled culture forward in a rickshaw. Tomorrow it will be its chauffeur who observes, thinks and steers instead of running and sweating.

The machine is the liberation of people from the slave labor era. Through machines, a mind can do more work and create more value than millions of hands. The machine is materialized human spirit. The grateful creation of man, begotten by the spirit of the inventor, born of the physical strength of the workers.

The machine has a double task: to increase production and reduce labor.

By increasing production, the machine will meet needs, by reducing the labor, end slavery.

Today, workers may only be the least part human, because he must be largely machine. In the future, the machine will perform the mechanical work and leave the human, the organic, to the humans. This is how the machine opens up the prospect of raising human work to an intellectual and individual plane: the free and creative component will grow over the automatic-mechanical, the spiritual versus the material. Only then will work stop to depersonalize, mechanize and degrade people; then work will be similar to play, sports, and free, creative activity. She will not, as today, be captor that oppresses everything human, but a tool against boredom, a distraction and physical or mental exercise for the development of all of his abilities. This work, which man will perform as the brain of his machine and which is based on domination, will stimulate instead of dull, lift up instead of depress.

3. DISMANTLING THE BIG CITY

In addition to these two tasks, alleviating need by increasing productivity and dismantling slavery by reducing and individualizing work, the machine has a third, cultural mission: the dissolution of the modern metropolis and the return of man to nature.

The origins of the modern metropolis came at a time when the horse was the fastest means of transport and there was no telephone. At that time, it was necessary for people to live in close proximity to their workplaces, and as a result lived in a cramped space.

Technology has changed these conditions: fast train, car, bicycle and the telephone allow the worker today to live many miles away from his office. There is no need for the construction of for the construction and accumulation of rental barracks. In the future, people will have the opportunity to live next to each other, instead of on top of each other, breathing healthy air in gardens, and living healthy, clean, decent lives in bright and spacious rooms. Electric and gas ovens will protect against the winter cold, electric lamps against the long winter nights. The human spirit will triumph over the winter and make the northern zone just as comfortable as the moderate one.

The development towards the garden city has already begun. The rich are leaving the centers of the big cities and settle on their periphery or their surroundings. The new industrial cities are expanding horizontally instead of vertically. At a higher level, the cities of the future will be somewhat similar to those of the Middle Ages. As the low civic houses were grouped around a huge cathedral, thus will be a huge skyscraper (which will include all public and private offices and dining hall) surrounded by the low houses and wide gardens of the garden city. In industrialized cities, the factory will be the central cathedral of work: the devotion of the people in these cathedrals of the future will be the work for the community.

Those not tied to the city by profession will live in the countryside and take part in the conveniences, activities and diversions of the cities through long-distance services and wireless connections.

There will come a time when people will not understand how it was once possible to live in the stone labyrinths we now know as modern big cities. The ruins will then be admired, as today the caves of the cave dwellers. Doctors will scratch their heads, how it was possible, from the standpoint of hygiene, that people could live and thrive in such an environment, closed off from nature, freedom, light and air, in such an atmosphere of soot, smoke, dust and dirt.

The coming downsizing of the big city as a consequence of the upturn in traffic engineering is a necessary precondition for real culture. Because in the unnatural and unhealthy atmosphere of today's big city, people are systematically poisoned and crippled—body, soul and spirit. The urban culture is a marsh plant because it is borne by degenerate, morbid and decadent people who have voluntarily or involuntarily fallen into this dead-end life.

4. THE CULTURAL PARADISE OF THE MILLIONAIRE

Technology is able to offer modern human beings more happiness and possibilities than past years offered their princes and kings.

Of course, at the beginning of the technological world period, the number of those to whom the inventions of the modern age are available is still small.

A modern millionaire can surround himself with luxury, comfort and beauty the world has to offer. He can enjoy all the fruits of nature and culture, and can live without working where and how he likes. By phone or car, he can choose to be connected with the world, or not; he can live as a hermit in the big city or in society on his country estate; he does not have to suffer either from the climate or from overpopulation; hunger and frost are alien to him; through his airplane he is master of the sky, through his yacht lord of the seas. In many ways he is freer and more powerful than Napoleon and Caesar. They could only control humans, but they could not fly over oceans and communicate across continents. He, on the other hand, is the lord of nature. Forces of nature serve him like invisible, mighty servants and spirits. With their help, he can fly faster and higher than a bird, drive faster over the earth than a gazelle and live under water like a fish. Through these abilities and powers he is even freer than the native of the South Seas and has overcome the biblical course. On the road through culture he has returned to a more perfect paradise.

The basis for such a fulfilled life has been created by technology. For the chosen few, technology has turned the forests and swamps into a cultural paradise. In these lucky children, man can see the promise of destiny for his grandchildren. They are the vanguard of mankind on their way into the garden of Eden of the future. What is exceptional today, can, with more technical progress, become the rule. Technology has busted the gates of paradise; only a few have passed through the narrow entrance so far, but the way is open and through diligence and spirit all humanity can follow these lucky children. Man does not need to despair; he has never been so close to his goal as he is today.

Just a few centuries ago, the possession of a glass window, mirror, clock, soap or sugar was a great luxury:

technology has spread these once rare commodities over the masses. Just as everyone today wears a watch and owns a mirror, so maybe in a century or so every person could have a car, his own villa and his own telephone. Prosperity has to increase all the more quickly and become more common, the faster the production numbers increase in relation to the population numbers. It is the cultural goal of technology to offer to all people the opportunities in life that today are available to those millionaires. That is why technology is fighting against necessity, not against wealth. Against bondage, not against domination. The goal is wealth, power, leisure, beauty and happiness for everyone. Not proletarianization, but aristocratization of humanity.

VIII. SPIRIT OF THE TECHNOLOGICAL AGE

1. HEROIC PACIFISM

The paradise of the future will not be won by coups. It can only be conquered by work. The spirit of the technological age is heroic-pacifistic: heroic, because technology is war with a changed weapon, pacifist, because the battle is not directed against people but against nature.

The technological heroism is bloodless: the hero works, thinks, acts and dares, not seeking to take the life of his fellow man, but to release him from the slavery of hunger, cold, distress and forced labor.

The hero of the technological age is a peaceful hero of work and intellect.

The work of the technological age is asceticism: self-control and self-sacrifice. In its present form and extent, it is not a pleasure, but a hard sacrifice we offer to our fellow human beings and our descendants.

Asceticism means exercise: it is the Greek expression for what in English is "training"; through this translation, the word "asceticism" loses its pessimistic character and becomes optimistic-heroic.

The optimistic, life-affirming asceticism of the technological age is preparing god's kingdom on earth: clearing the earth for paradise; for this purpose, it moves mountains, rivers and lakes, wraps the globe in wires and rails, creates plantations from forests and farmland from steppes. Like a supernatural being, man is changing the surface of the earth according to his needs.

2. THE SPIRIT OF LAZINESS

In the age of work and technology, there is no greater vice than laziness, as in the age of war, there is no greater vice than cowardice.

The overcoming of inertia is the main task of technological heroism.

Where life manifests as energy, inertia is the sign of death. The struggle of life against death is a struggle of energy against inertia. The victory of death over life is a victory of inertia over energy. The messengers of death are old age and disease. In them, inertia wins over the life force: limbs and movements get limp. Vitality, courage and joy of living sink; everything tilts to the ground, gets tired and lethargic, until the man, who can no longer move forward and can not stand up, sinks into the grave as a victim of lethargy; there inertia triumphs over life.

All young flowers grow, against gravity, towards the sun: all ripe fruits fall, overwhelmed by gravity, to the earth.

The symbol of technology's victory over gravity, of human will and human spirit over the inertia of matter is the flying man. Few things are as sublime and as beautiful as he. Poetry and truth, romance and technology, the mythologies of Daedalus and Wieland are married here with the visions of Leonardo and Goethe. Through the actions of scientists, the wildest dreams of poetry become reality: on wings stretched by his mind and will, man rises above space, time and gravity, over the earth and the sea.

3. BEAUTY AND TECHNOLOGY

Anyone who still doubts the beauty of technology is silenced in the face of the flying man. But not only the plane gives us new beauty: the automobile, motorboat, fast locomotive, generator have their own specific beauty of action and movement. But because this beauty is dynamic, it cannot, like the static beauty of the landscape, be held in place by brush, stylus and chisel: therefore, it does not exist for people who have no original sense of beauty, which art uses as a guide in the maze of beauty's garden.

A thing is beautiful by the ideal of harmony and vitality that it conveys to us and the impulses we have in their direction. Each culture creates its own symbols of power and beauty: the Greek increased his own harmony in the statues and temples; the Roman increased his strength in circus fights of predators and gladiators; the medieval Christian deepened and transfigured his soul through the love of sacrifices and sacraments; the modern citizen grew up with the heroes of his theaters and novels; the Japanese learned about grace and destiny from his flowers.

In a time of restless progress, the ideal of beauty had to become dynamic, and with it its symbol. The man of the technological age is a student of the machine he has created: from it he learns tireless activity and concentrated power. The machine as creature and temple of holy human spirit symbolizes the overcoming of matter by the mind, of the static by movement, of laziness by power: getting up in the service of an idea, liberating humanity through action.

Technology has gifted the coming age a new form of expression: the cinema. Cinema is about to replace today's theater, yesterday's church, circus and amphitheater of the day before yesterday, and to play a leading role in the culture of the working state of the future.

In all of its artistic deficiencies, film is already beginning to unconsciously carry a new gospel to the masses: the gospel of power and beauty. It announces beyond good and evil, the victory of the strongest man and the most beautiful woman, whether the man surpasses his rival in bodily, will, or intellectual power, adventurer or hero, criminal or detective, and whether the woman is sexier or nobler, more gracious or selfless than the others, a courtesan or mother. The screen screams to the men in thousands of variations: "Be strong!" To the women: "Be beautiful!"

To purify and expand this mission of mass education that slumbers in cinema is one of today's artists biggest and most important tasks, because the cinema of the future will undoubtedly have a greater influence on the proletarian (working class) culture than theater had on the bourgeois.

4. EMANCIPATION

The cult of the technological age is a cult of power. There is no time and leisure for the development of harmony. In its name will be the golden age of culture, which will follow the iron age of work.

Typical for the dynamic attitude of our age is its male-European character. Nietzsche's male-European ethics are our time's protest against the feminine-Asian morality of Christianity.

The emancipation of women is also a symptom of the masculinization of our world, because it does not lead the feminine type to power, but the masculine. While in the past the feminine woman by her influence on the man participated in world leadership, today "men" of both sexes wield the scepter of economic and political power. The emancipation of women signifies the triumph of the "man-woman" over the real, feminine woman; it does not lead to the victory, but to the abolition of women. The "lady" is already extinct: the "woman" should follow her. Through emancipation, the female sex, which has been partially excluded, is being mobilized for the technological war and placed in the army of labor.

The emancipation of Asians takes place under the same conditions as the emancipation of women; it is a symptom of the Europeanization of our world: because it does not lead the Asian type to victory, but the European. While in the past the Asian spirit dominated Europe through Christianity, today white and colored Europeans share world domination. The so-called Orient's Awakening means the triumph of the yellow European over the true Oriental; it does not lead to the victory, but to the destruction of Asian culture. Where the blood of Asia triumphs in the East, the spirit of Europe wins with it: the masculine, hard, dynamic, purposeful, active, rational mind. In order to participate in progress, Asia must replace its harmonious soul and culture with the European. The emancipation of the Asians means their entry into the European-American army of work and their mobilization for the war of technology. After its completion, Asia will again be Asian, and women will be able to be feminine again: then Asia and women will educate the world in a purer harmony. Until then, however, Asians will have to wear the European uniform, women the male.

5. CHRISTIANITY AND KNIGHTHOOD

Anyone who understands culture as harmony with nature must call our era barbaric; anyone who understands culture as confrontation with nature recognizes the specific, masculine-European form of our culture. The Christian-Asian origin of European ethics made us misunderstand the ethical value of the progress of technology; it is only under the perspective of Nietzsche that the heroic-ascetic struggle of the technological age for salvation through mind and work appears as good and noble.

The virtues of the technological age are, above all: energy, perseverance, bravery, renunciation, self-control and solidarity. These qualities steel the soul to the bloodless, hard fight of social work.

The ethic of work follows the knightly ethics of battle: both are male, both Nordics. Now this ethic will adapt to new conditions and put a new work honor in place of the surviving knightly honor. The new concept of honor will be based on work—the new shame on laziness. The lazy person will be considered and despised as a deserter of the working front. The objects of the new hero worship will be inventors, instead of barons: value creators instead of value destroyers.

From the Christian morality, the ethic of work will take over the spirit of pacifism and socialism: because only peace is productive for technological progress, and war is destructive, and because only the social spirit of cooperation of all creators can lead to technology's victory over nature.

6. THE BUDDHIST DANGER

Any passivist and hostile propaganda against the technological and industrial development is treason against the army of the European work force: because it is a call for retreat and desertion during the deciding campaign. Tolstoians and neo-Buddhists are guilty of this cultural crime: they challenge mankind to surrender to nature shortly before the final victory, to evacuate the terrain conquered by technology and voluntarily return to the primitiveness of agriculture and cattle breeding. Tired of the battle, they want Europe to live a poor, childish existence instead of creating a new world through the highest application of the mind, will and muscles.

That which still is viable and vital in Europe rejects this cultural suicide: it senses the uniqueness of its situation and its responsibility to future generations. Laying down the weapons of technology would throw the world back into the Asian culture cycle. The technological world revolution which is called Europe, would collapse and bury one of the greatest hopes of mankind. Europe, which lives from its heroic creations, must inwardly reject the spirit of Buddhism. Japan, as it becomes more industrialized, must internally reject Buddhism; so, the more Europe internally submits to Buddhism, it must neglect and betray its technological mission. Buddhism is a wonderful crowning for mature cultures, but a dangerous poison for nascent cultures. Its worldview is good for old age, for autumn—as the religion of Nietzsche is for youth and spring—Goethe's belief is for the bloom of summer.

Buddhism would suffocate technology, and with it, the spirit of Europe.

Europe should remain true to its mission and never deny the roots of its nature: heroism and rationalism, Germanic will and Hellenistic spirit. Because the miracle that is Europe arose from the marriage of these two elements. The blind drive of the Nordic barbarians became seeing and fruitful through contact with the spiritual culture of the middle European nations: so, warriors became thinkers, heroes became inventors.

Asia's mysticism threatens Europe's mental clarity; Asia's passivism threatens its male energy. Only if Europe resists these temptations and dangers and remembers its Hellenic and Germanic ideals, will it be able to fight the battle of technology to the end, to redeem itself and the world.

IX. STINNES AND KRASSIN

1. ECONOMIC STATES

Stinnes is the leader of the capitalist economy of Germany—Krassin is the leader of the communist economy of Russia. In the following they are considered as exponents of capitalist and communist production, not as personalities.

Since the collapse of the three major European military monarchies, there are only economic states left in our part of the world: economic problems are at the center of internal and external politics: Mercury rules the world, as the heir of Mars—as a forerunner of Apollo.

The transformation from the military state to the economic state is the political expression of the fact that, instead of the war front, the labor front has moved into the foreground of history.

Military states correspond to the age of war—economic states correspond to the age of labor.

The communist as well as the capitalist state are labor states, no longer war states—not yet culture states. Both are characterized by production and by progress. Both are ruled by producers, as once the military states were ruled by militaries: the communist by the leaders of the industrial workers, the capitalist by the leaders of the industrialists.

Capitalism and communism are just as much related to one another as are Catholicism and Protestantism, which for centuries thought of themselves as extreme opposites and fought bloodily. Not their difference, but their kinship is the cause of the bitter hatred with which they persecute each other.

As long as capitalists and communists hold the view that it is permissible and imperative to kill or starve people for advocating different economic principles, they are both at a very low level of ethical development. Theoretically, of course, the premises and goals of communism are more ethical than those of capitalism, because they are based on more objective and fairer points of view.

However, ethical considerations are not decisive for technological progress: here the decisive question is whether the capitalist or the communist system is more rational and more appropriate to carry out technology's liberation war against the forces of nature.

2. THE RUSSIAN FIASCO

The success speaks for Stinnes, against Krassin: capitalist economy is flourishing, while the communist is at a standstill. To deduce the value of the two systems from this statement would be simply unfair. For it must not be overlooked under which circumstances Communism took over and led the Russian economy: after a military-, political- and social collapse, after the loss of important industrial areas, in a fight against the whole world, under pressure of years of a blockade, continuous civil war and passive resistance by farmers, civilians and intelligentsia; to this was added the catastrophic crop failure. If one considers all these circumstances, as well as the lower organizational talent and education of the Russian people, one can only marvel that some of the Russian industry has survived.

To compare the failure of the five-year old communism with the success of the mature capitalism under these circumstances, would be just as unfair as comparing a newborn child to an adult man and then determining that the child was is idiot—while in him, maybe, sleeps a genius.

Even if communism in Russia collapses, it would be equally naïve to declare the revolution a thing of the past—just as it would have been foolish after the collapse of the Hussite movement to believe the reformation was over: because after a few decades Luther appeared and led many of the Hussite ideas to victory.

3. CAPITALIST AND COMMUNIST PRODUCTION

The essential advantage of the capitalist economy lies in its experience. It controls all methods of organization and production, all strategic secrets in the struggle between man and nature, and has a staff of trained industrial officers. Communism, on the other hand, is forced to design new war plans with an inadequate general staff and officer staff, to try new methods of organization and production. Stinnes can advance on known tracks, while Krassin must be a scout in the jungle of the economic revolution.

Through competition, profit and risk, capitalism owns an unsurpassable engine that keeps the economic apparatus in constant motion: egoism. Every entrepreneur, inventor, engineer, and worker in the capitalist state is constantly harnessing its forces to avoid being overrun by competition and going under. The soldiers and officers of the labor army must advance so as to not get under the wheels.

In the free initiative of a company is another advantage of capitalism, to which technology owes a lot. One of the most difficult problems of communism is the avoidance of the economic bureaucracy by which it is constantly threatened.

The main technical advantage of communism lies in the fact that it has the opportunity to combine all the productive forces and natural resources of its economic area and to rationally use them according to a uniform plan. In doing so, he saves all the forces that capitalism is wasting on defending against the competition. The basic systematic nature of the communist economy, which today undertakes to rationalize the Russian empire in accordance with a unified plan, technically represents a substantial advantage over the Capitalist production anarchy. The Communist labor army fights under one united command against the hostile nature, while the fragmented labor battalions of capitalism not only fight against the common enemy, but also against each other, to deafeat the competition. In addition, Krassin holds his army firmer in his hand than Stinnes, because the workers of the Stinnes army are aware that part of their work is for the enrichment of a foreign, hostile enterprise, while the Krassin army are aware that they work for the communist state, of which they are partners and supporters. Stinnes appears to his workers as oppressor and adversary, Krassin as leader and associate. Therefore, Krassin can dare to ban strikes and introduce Sunday work, while for Stinnes this would be impossible.

The Stinnes army is decomposed by growing dissatisfaction and mutiny, while the Krassin army, despite its material needs, is supported by an "ideal" goal. In short, the war against the forces of nature is a civil war in Russia, whereas in Europe and America it is a dynastic war of industry kings.

The labor of the communist worker is a battle for his state and his form of state—the labor of the capitalist worker is a battle for his life. Here, the main driving force behind labor is egoism—there it is *political idealism.* Unfortunately, at the present state of ethics, egoism is a stronger motor than idealism, and thus the fighting value of the capitalist labor army is greater than that of the communist. Communism has a more rational economic plan—capitalism has a stronger work engine.

Capitalism will fail, not because of its technical, but because of its ethical defects. The discontent of Stinnes' army will not be held down by rifles in the long run. Pure capitalism is based on the dependence and ignorance of the workers—like the slave obedience of the military. The more independent, self-confident and educated the working class becomes, the more impossible it will be for private individuals to make them work for their private interests.

The future belongs to Krassin—the Russian experiment will decide today's economy. That is why it is in the best interest of the whole world not only not to disturb this experiment, but to strongly support it. Because only then would its outcome be an answer to the question of whether communism is capable of reforming today's economy—or whether the necessary evil of capitalism is preferable to it.

4. MERCENARIES AND SOLDIERS OF LABOR

Capitalism corresponds to the mercenary army in the age of war—communism to the people's army. In the time of mercenaries, every wealthy man could recruit and equip a military army, which he salaried and commanded—just as today every rich man can recruit and equip a labor army, which he salaries and commands.

Three centuries ago, Wallenstein played an analogous role in Germany, as Stinnes today: with the help of his fortune, which he had multiplied in the Bohemian war, and the army which he promoted and maintained, Wallenstein transformed from a private man to the most powerful personality of the German Reich—just as Stinnes today through his fortune, which he increased in the world war, as well as through the press and a labor army, which he promotes and maintains, became the most powerful man in the German Republic.

In the capitalist state, the worker is a mercenary, the entrepreneur is the commander—in the communist state, the worker is a soldier, which is subordinate to the state-controlled generals. As the commanders conquered and built dynasties with the blood of their mercenaries, so the modern commanders conquer with the sweat of their laborers wealth and power and build plutocratic dynasties.

As every mercenary commander then, so industry leaders today negotiate as equals with governments and states: they influence politics with their money, as they once did with their power.

The reform of the labor army, which is carried out by communism, corresponds in all details to the reform of the army, which all the modern states have undergone.

The army reform has replaced the mercenary armies with people's armies: it introduced mandatory enrollment, nationalized the army, banned private recruitment, replaced the landowners with state-employed officers and ethically glorified the military.

The labor state is introducing the same reforms in the labor army: it proclaims mandatory labor, nationalizes the industry, bans private enterprise, replaces the private entrepreneurs with state-appointed directors and glorifies work as a moral duty.

Stinnes and Krassin are both commanders of mighty labor forces fighting against the common enemy: the Nordic nature. Stinnes leads a mercenary army as a modern Wallenstein—Krassin leads a people's army as field marshal of a labor state. While these two leaders consider themselves opponents, they are allies, marching separate, strike as one.

5. SOCIAL CAPITALISM—LIBERAL COMMUNISM

Just as the regeneration of Catholicism was a consequence of the reformation, so could the rivalry of capitalism and communism fertilize both: if, instead of fighting each other through murder, slander and sabotage, they would limit themselves to showing their higher worth through cultural achievements.

No theoretical justification of capitalism promotes this system more than the indisputable fact that the life of American workers (some of whom drive to work in their own car) is in fact better than that of the Russians, who are equally starving and starving to death. Because prosperity is more important than equality: it is better, all prosper and few get rich than that general, equal misery prevails. Only envy and pedantry can resist this judgement. Best, of course, would be universal, equal wealth—but that is in the future, not in the present: it can only be brought about by technology, not politics.

American capitalism is aware that it can only hold its own through generous social action. It considers itself a trustee of the national wealth, which it uses to promote inventions, cultural and humanitarian purposes.

Only a social capitalism that makes such an effort to reconcile with the workforce has a chance of survival: only a liberal communism that seeks to reconcile with the intelligentsia has a chance of survival. England is trying the first route, Russia the second. Conducting a war against the will of the officers is just as impossible in the long run as it is against the will of the troops. This also applies to the labor army: it depends on expert leaders as well as on willing workers.

Krassin realized that it is necessary for communism to learn from capitalism. That is why he recently promoted the private initiative, appointing to heads of state-owned enterprises energetic and expert engineers with the broadest authority and profit sharing, and brought back part of the displaced industrialists; finally, he supports the weak engine of idealism with egoism, ambition and coercion, and through this mixed system seeks to increase the work performance of the Russian proletariat.

Only these capitalist methods can save communism: Krassin has come to realize that winter and the drought are crueler Russian despots than all the tsars and grand dukes: that the more decisive war of liberation applies to them. That is why today he is focusing on combating hunger, on electricity and the rebuilding of industry and railways, even sacrificing a series of political principles for these technical plans. He knows that his economic success or failure will determine his political and that it will depend on him whether the Russian revolution eventually leads to the world's solution, or the world's disappointment.

By the current state of ethics, the abolition of private property will fail due to insurmountable psychological resistance. Nevertheless, communism remains a turning point in economic development of the entrepreneurial state to the worker's state, as well as the political evolution from the barren system of plutocratic democracy to a new social aristocracy of intelligent people.

6. CORPORATION AND UNIONS

As long as communism proves too immature to lead the technological liberation battle, Krassin and Stinnes will have to come to an understanding. This way of cooperation instead of working against each other will be rejected by the fanatical fools of capitalism and communism: only the best heads of both camps will meet in the realization that it is better to save world culture by peace of understanding, than to destroy it by a violent victory. Then the commanders of the mercenaries will become the generals of economy, and the mercenaries, soldiers.

In tomorrow's "red" economy there cannot be equality between the leaders and the led: but future industrialists will no longer be as irresponsible as they are today—but feel responsible for the community. Unproductive industrialists (dealers) will vanish from the economic life just as once the decorated court generals vanished from the army. As is often the case today, the productive capitalist will have to become the most intensive worker in his factory. By simultaneously reducing his excess profits, a fair balance will be made between his work and his income.

Two groups of economic forces are beginning to share in the leadership of the economy in the capitalist worker's state: the representatives of the entrepreneurs and of the workers. Corporations and unions. Their influence on politics is growing and will outstrip the importance of parliaments. They will complement and control each other like the senate and tribunate, upper house and lower house. The conquest of natural forces and capture of natural resources will be led by corporations—the distribution of the spoils controlled by the unions.

On a common ground of production increase and perfection of technology, Stinnes and Krassin will meet: they are opponents in the question of distribution, but fellows in the question of production: they fight against each other in the question of the economic method—fight together in the people's war against the forces of nature.

X. FROM WORKER STATE TO CULTRURE STATE

1. CHILD WORSHIP

Our age is at the same time an epoch of technology and of culture. It has two demands:

—Expansion of the Worker State

—Preparation of the Culture State

The first task puts politics in the service of technology—the second in the service of ethics. Only the focus on the coming age of culture gives the suffering and struggling humanity of the technological age the strength to continue the battle against the forces of nature to victory.

The extra work done by modern man is his legacy to the people of the future; through this extra work, he accumulates a capital of knowledge, machines and values whose interest his grandchildren will enjoy.

The division of humanity into masters and slaves, into culture bearers and forced laborers, is recognized today. But these classes are starting to shift from social to temporal. We are not the slaves of our contemporaries, but of our grandchildren. Instead of juxtaposed slave and master classes, our culture is based on a succession of masters and slaves. Today's working world sets the foundation for tomorrow's world of culture.

As once cultural pleasure of the lords was built on the overwork by slaves, so the cultural enjoyment of the future will be built on present overwork. The present population is in the service of the coming; we sow so that others may reap; our time works, researches and struggles for a future world to emerge in beauty.

Thus, worship of children takes the place of the Eastern ancestor worship. It flourishes in the capitalist as well as the communist labor state: in America as in Russia. The world kneels before the child as an idol, as the promise of a better future. It has become a dogma to consider first the child in all charity. In the Capitalist West, fathers work themselves to death to leave their children richer opportunities in life. In the Communist East, an entire generation is living and dying in misery to ensure a happier and more just future for their descendants. The European age is devoted to the future.

Western child worship is rooted in the belief in evolution. The European regards the newer as better, more sophisticated; he believes that his grandchildren will be worthier of freedom than he and his contemporaries: he believes that the world is moving forward. While the Oriental sees the present balanced between past and future, it appears to the European as a rolling ball, which freed from the past rushes to an unknown future. The Asian is beyond time; the European moves with time: he rejects his past and embraces his future. His story is a constant statement about the past and push for the future. Because he feels the progress of time, standstill for him means a step backwards. He lives in a Herculean world of becoming; the Asian lives in the Parmenidean world of being.

As a result of this view, our age can only be judged from the perspective of the coming one. It is a time of preparation and battle, immaturity and transition. We are a young generation that strides across the bridge between two worlds and stands at the beginning of an unrestrained cultural circle. We feel the most when we move forward, grow and fight—not in the peaceful enjoyment of Oriental maturity. Our goal is not pleasure, but freedom; tranquility is not our road, but action.

2. MANDATORY LABOR

The expansion of the labor state is a cultural obligation of our age. The labor state is the last stage of man on his way to the cultural paradise of the future.

Expanding the labor state means: to put all available forces of nature and of man in the most rational way at the service of production and technological progress.

In an age that is building the foundations of future cultures, nobody has the right to leisure. Mandatory labor is an ethical and technical duty at the same time.

Popper-Lynkeus has designed an ideal program for the development of the labor state in his work, "A Guaranteed Subsistence for All". He demands that compulsory military service be replaced by compulsory labor service. This would last more years and would enable the state to guarantee to all its members a minimum of food, housing, clothing, heating and medical care throughout their lives. This program could end the misery and worry and at the same time the dictatorship of the capitalists and proletarians. Class differences would cease as a result of mandatory labor, as the difference between professional soldiers and civilians ceased as a result of mandatory military service. The abolition of the proletariat, however, is a more desirable ideal than its regulation.

Universal mandatory labor is the price that Popper-Lynkeus demands for the elimination of misery and worry. Reducing this mandatory labor to a minimum by improving technology and organization—and eventually replacing it with voluntary labor, forms the second stage of the work state.

The hope which Lenin expresses in "State and Revolution" that people would continue to work voluntarily even after the abolition of mandatory labor is no utopia for Northerners. Because the restless European and American finds no satisfaction in inactivity; through several thousand years of necessity, work has become second nature to him; he needs it to exercise his powers and ban the ghosts of boredom. His ideal is action—not contemplation. For this reason—not out of greed—most millionaires in the West continue to work restlessly instead of enjoying their wealth. For the same reason, many employees consider their retirement as a shock; they prefer their usual work to forced leisure.

In the current state of technology, voluntary work would be insufficient to supply all the necessities: still much overwork and mandatory labor are necessary to clear the road for a beautiful and free work of the future.

Inventors pave the way into the future. Their tireless and quiet labor is more essential and meaningful to the culture than the loud politicians and artists who are pushing into the foreground of the world arena. Modern society is obliged to promote its inventors and their activities in every conceivable way: it should grant them the privileged position that the Middle Ages granted to monks and priests, thus offering them the opportunity to invent without worries.

Inventors are the most important personalities of our time; industrial workers are their pillars; they are the forerunners in humanity's struggle for sovereignty, giving birth to the creations begotten by invention.

3. PRODUCER—AND CONSUMER STATE

Another duty of the labor state is to raise general prosperity by increasing production.

As soon as more food is thrown in the market than can be consumed, hunger stops, and the blissful state of the country returns at a higher level.

Only when the city builds more flats than it houses families can it banish the housing shortage, which it only relieves, redistributes and shifts through forced housing.

Only when as many cars are being produced as pocket watches, every worker becomes a car owner: not by giving the commissioners confiscated cars of bank directors.

Only through production, not through confiscation, can the prosperity of a people continually increase.

In the capitalist state, production depends on pricing. If it is in the interest of pricing, the producer is just as determined to destroy his products as to produce them, to inhibit technology as to promote it, to reduce production as to increase it. If technological and cultural progress is consistent with his interests, he is ready to promote them; if they conflict with each other, he has no qualms about choosing profits over technology, production and culture. It is in the constant interest of producers that demand always exceeds supply, while it is in the interest of consumers that supply exceeds demand.

The producer lives off the consumer's need: grain producers live off the fact that people are starving; coal producers live off the fact that people are freezing. They have an interest in perpetuating hunger and frost. The bread industry would sabotage the invention of a bread substitute, the coal industry, the invention of a coal substitute; they would also try to buy and destroy such inventions. The workers in the relevant sectors would be in solidarity with the companies so as not to lose work and income.

The industrialists and workers are interested in higher prices for their industrial products, the farmers and farm workers in higher prices for their farm products. As producers, the desires of the people diverge, whereas as consumers, all people have the same, common goal: reducing prices by increasing production.

Another mischief of the "producer state" is advertisement. It is a necessary consequence of competition and consists of an increase in demand through artificial advertising of human desire. To showcase and impose luxury, which awakens desire without ever being able to satisfy it, it acts as the main cause of general envy, general dissatisfaction and bitterness. No city dweller can buy all the goods that blind his eyes in the displays: he therefore always feels poor, relative to the exhibited riches and pleasures. The spiritual devastation caused by advertisement can only be eliminated by abolishing competition; competition can only be eliminated by turning away from capitalism.

In spite of the great advancement that the technological age owes to capitalism, it must not be blinded to the threats from this side: it must bring about a better system in time to avoid the mistakes of capitalism.

The rival and heir of the capitalist entrepreneur state—the communist "labor state"—contains a part of the mistakes of its predecessor, because even in it there is a group of producers; it too is a producer state.

The culture state of the future, on the other hand, will be a consumer state: its production will be controlled by the consumer, not, as it is today, the consumer by the producers. Production will not be for profit, but for the sake of the general welfare and culture: not for the sake of the producers, but the consumers.

It is the future mission of the parliament to represent the common interests of all consumers, whose mouthpieces today are still the representatives and parties.

4. REVOLUTION AND TECHNOLOGY

The overthrow of the economy that is supposed to transform Europe's current production anarchy into a new order must never forget its productive mission and must be on guard not to fall into the destructive methods of Russia. Because of its northern location and overpopulation, Europe is more dependent on organized labor and production. It cannot, even temporarily live on the alms of its stingy nature; everything it has achieved, it owes to the deeds of its labor army. Radical disorganization through war or anarchy would mean the cultural death of Europe: because a temporary standstill of European production would mean that one-hundred million Europeans would starve to death; Europe, which lacks the resilience of Russia, could not survive such a catastrophe. Ethics demand of the coming overthrow of Europe that it protects and sanctifies human life; technology demands of the coming overthrow of Europe that it protects and sanctifies human creations.

Anyone who willfully kills a human being sins against the holy spirit of the community; anyone who willfully destroys a machine sins against the holy spirit of labor. Capitalism was guilty of this double crime in the world war, communism in the Russian revolution. Neither revered human life or human labor.

If Europe is teachable, it can learn from the Russian revolution which methods it should not use, because it has a warning about the importance of technology and the revenge it takes on its detractors. Russia's leaders thought that they could save their country and the world through ethical goals and military means alone, rather than through work and technology. They sacrificed the industry and technology of their country for politics. As they reached for the stars, they lost the ground of production under their feet and fell into the abyss of misery. In order to save themselves from this abyss in which Russian peoples are deteriorating, the communist leaders are forced to ask their mortal capitalist enemies for help against the overpowering Russian climate, which once shattered Napoleon's great army and today threatens Bolshevism with the same fate.

If Europe follows the destructive example of the Russian revolution, it risks, instead of establishing a new, postcapitalism order, sinking back into the primitiveness of pre-capitalist barbarism and being forced to relive the capitalist era. Clear-mindedness may protect it from this tragic fate: otherwise it will be like a patient who dies of heart failure from anesthesia, while an operation is being performed of him. Because the heartbeat of Europe is technology: without technology it cannot live, even under the freest constitution. Before the distribution of goods can be improved, the production of goods must be secured, because what use is equality if everyone starves to death? And what harm is inequality when no one is suffering?

The European revolution would have to multiply its production instead of destroying it—reviving its technology instead of destroying it. Only then would it have the prospect of success and permanent realization of its ethical ideals.

The organization and machinery of Europe forms the basis of its future culture. If Europe tries to set up the political roof of this cultural construction, before the technological foundations, the construction collapses and buries the frivolous architects along with the unfortunate residents.

5. DANGERS OF TECHNOLOGY

The course of the Russian revolution has shown where ethical demands lead, if they are blind to technological needs. The course of the World War has shown where technological advances lead, when they are blind to ethical needs.

Technology without ethics must lead to catastrophes just as ethics without technology. If Europe makes no progress in ethical terms, it has to stumble from one world war to another: these will be the more terrible the higher technology develops. Europe's collapse is inevitable, if its ethical progress does not keep pace with its technological. Nevertheless, it would be equally ridiculous and cowardly to fight and condemn technology as such because of the possibility of technological and cultural disasters, as it would be to avoid and blame the railroad because of possibilities of railroad accidents.

While Europe is expanding the labor state, it must never forget to prepare the culture state: teachers and priests, artists and writers, prepare the people for a great feast that is the goal of technology. Their importance is as great as that of engineers, chemists and doctors: these shape the body of the coming culture, those shape the soul. Because technology is the body—ethics the soul of culture. Here lies their contrast and their relationship.

Ethics teach people the right use of the power and freedom that technology gives them. Abuse of power and freedom is more fatal to humans than powerlessness and un-freedom. Human malady could make life worse in the future era of leisure than in the present era of forced labor. It depends on ethics whether technology will lead people to hell or heaven. The machine is wearing the Head of Janus: if handled responsible, it becomes the slave-girl of future man and will provide him with power, freedom, leisure and culture—handled irresponsibly, the machine will enslave man and rob him of his remaining power and culture. If it is not possible to turn the machine into an organ of man, then man will sink to being a component of the machine.

Technology without ethics is "practical materialism": it leads to the downfall of man's humanity, and to his transformation into a machine; it misleads man to become an alien und give his soul to *things*. But all technological progress becomes harmful and worthless, when man, while conquering the world, loses his soul: it would be better if he had remained animal.

Just as armies and wars were once necessary for the preservation of freedom and culture among nations, labor and technology are necessary in poor and overpopulated parts of the world for the preservation of life and culture. But the army must defend political goals, technology ethics. A technology that emancipates itself from ethics and considers itself to be an end in itself is just as catastrophic for culture as it is for an army that emancipates itself from politics and considers itself an end in itself: a leaderless industrialism will tear down culture as much as a leaderless militarism destroys the state.

As the body is an organ of the soul, technology must submit to ethical leadership; it must be careful not to fall into the error which art has committed in proclaiming "art for art's sake". Neither art nor technology, nor science, nor politics are ends in themselves: they are ways to lead to humanity—a strong, complete human.

6. ROMANTICISM OF THE FUTURE

In times of hardship nostalgia grows, and with it, romanticism.

Even our time has given birth to romanticism: everywhere there is longing for foreign, more beautiful worlds, which are supposed to help us overcome the grey of our work day. The nurseries of modern romanticism: cinema, theaters and novels are like windows from which the forced laborers of the European penitentiary can look out into freedom.

Modern romanticism has four main forms:

The romance of the past that takes us back to the more colorful and freer ages of our history; the romance of distance that opens up the Great East and the Wild West; the romance of the occult, penetrating into the most intimate areas of life and soul and fill the bleakness of everyday life with wonders and secrets; the romance of the future, which consoles people by looking for a golden tomorrow.

Spengler, Kayserling und Steiner meet the modern romanticism: Spengler opens the cultures of the past, Kayserling the cultures of the distance, Steiner the riches of the Occult. The great influence that these men have on German intellectual life is partly due to the romantic longing of the heavily-tested German people, who look to the past, to the distance and to heaven, to find comfort there.

Imagination leads to the past, to the distance and to beyond, but action leads into the future. Therefor neither history, nor Orientalism, nor occultism works as the driving force of our time, but the romanticism of the future: it has given birth to the idea of the future state and thus to the world movement of socialism: it has conceived the idea of the superhuman and thus initiated the submission of values.

Marx, the herald of the future state and Nietzsche, the herald of the superhuman, are both romantics of the future.

They lay paradise neither in the past, nor in the distance, nor in the occult, but in the future.

Marx heralds the coming world empire of labor—Nietzsche the coming world culture. Everything that deals with the expansion of the labor state must consider socialism; everything that deals with the preparation of the culture state must consider the super human. Marx is the prophet of tomorrow, Nietzsche the prophet of the day after tomorrow.

All major social and intellectual events of modern Europe somehow tie to the works of these two men: the social and political revolution stands in the sign of Marx—the ethical and mental world revolution in the sign of Nietzsche. Without these two men, the face of Europe would look different.

Marx and Nietzsche, the heralds of social and individual future ideals, are both European, men, and dynamic forces. Their ideals will have to be realized through actions in the future. Their dynamic ideals contain demands: they not only want to teach, but force men; they turn man's eyes forward and thus they act as creators of society and of men. Their polarity reflects the essence of the European spirit and the future of European destiny.

The highest, ultimate ideal of European romanticism of the future is not turning away, but returning to nature on a higher level. Culture, ethics and technology are in the service of this ideal. After hundreds of thousands of years of war, human beings should once again make peace with nature and return home to her empire—but not as her creature, but as her master. Because man is about to overthrow the constitution of his planet: yesterday it was anarchistic, tomorrow it shall be monarchic. One among the billion creatures reaches for the crown of creation: the free, evolved human being as king of the earth.

PACIFISM—1924

To the dead, living, coming heroes of peace!

1. TEN YEARS OF WAR

The peace, which fell into ruins ten years ago, has not been restored to this day. The five-year war period was followed by a five-year semi-war period for Europe. The Russian-Polish and Greek-Turkish wars, Ruhr occupation, fighting in Upper Silesia, Lithuania, West Hungary, Fiume, Corfu, the civil wars in Germany, Italy, Spain, Hungary, Ireland, Greece, Bulgaria and Albania fall into this period, as well as the political murders and sedition, the collapse of currencies and the impoverishment of entire peoples.

This worst decade of European history since the migration is a worse indictment against the war than pacifists could ever issue: nevertheless, this defendant has not been punished, but can be celebrated everywhere as triumphant, dictates European politics, prepares to attack the peoples of Europe anew, and to finally destroy them.

Undoubtedly, as a result of the advance of technology of war—especially the manufacture of poison and aviation, the next European war would not weaken this part of the earth, but destroy it.

This danger, which affects him personally, must be taken into account by every European. If it appears inevitable to him, the emigration to a foreign part of the earth remains the logical consequence. If it appears avoidable to him, the fight against the danger of war and its carriers remains his duty—the duty to pacifism.

Today, staying European is not just a fate, but also a responsible task, on the solution of which depends the future of each and every one of us.

Pacifism is the only "realpolitik" in Europe today. Hoping for salvation through war is giving in to romantic illusions.

The majority of European politicians seem to recognize this and wish for peace, and with them the overwhelming majority of Europeans.

This fact cannot reassure the pacifist, who remembers that this was also the case in 1914; then, most of the statesmen and the majority of Europeans wanted peace. And yet, against their will, the war broke out. This outbreak of war was the result of an international coup d'état by the war-friendly minorities against the anti-war majorities.

This state seized on a favorable occasion, and with lies and slogans surprised unsuspecting peoples, whose destiny was left to those minorities for years.

The World War was the result of the militarists' determination and the pacifists' weakness. As long as this relationship remains, a new European war could break out any day. Today, as then, a small but energetic pro-war minority faces a large but powerless majority of peace; it plays with the war instead of crushing it: it appeases the warmongers instead of overthrowing them, thus creating the same situation as in 1914.

Pacifism forgets that a wolf is stronger than a thousand sheep—and that in politics as well as strategy numbers only decide if they are well managed and organized.

It is what pacifism lacks today as it did ten years ago. Had pacifism been better managed and organized then, the war would not have broken out; would it be today, Europe would be safe from a new war.

The powerlessness of pacifism lies, as it did then, in the fact that many wish for peace, but very few want it; many fear war, but only few fight it.

2. CITICISM OF PACIFISM

Passive war guilt affects European pacifism. Bad leadership, weakness and lack of character encouraged the warmongers to start the war.

The followers of the idea of peace, who in 1914 did not advocate for their ideal in time and not strongly enough, are partly responsible for the outbreak of war.

But if today, after this experience and knowledge, an opponent of war persists in his passivity, he invites an even heavier blame on himself by indirectly promoting a future war.

A rich pacifist who does not finance peace today is half warmonger.

A pacifist-minded journalist, who today does not propagate peace, is also a half war monger.

A voter who, for domestic-policy reasons, chooses a candidate whose commitment to peace he does not believe, signs a half death sentence for himself and his children.

The duty of every pacifist is: to make every feasible effort to prevent the treat of a future war; if he does not follow this direction, he is either not a pacifist or oblivious to his duties.

Pacifism learned nothing from the war: it is essentially the same today as in 1914. If it does not recognize its mistakes and does not change, militarism will continue to walk all over it in the future. The main mistakes of European pacifism are:

Pacifism is non-political: among its leaders are too many admirers and too few politicians. Therefore, pacifism is often based on illusions, does not count facts, human weakness, unreasonableness and malice; it draws wrong conclusions from wrong assumptions. Pacifism is boundless; it does not know how to limit its goals. It achieves nothing because it wants everything at the same time.

Pacifism is far-sighted; it is reasonable about the target, but unreasonable about the means. It directs its will towards the future, and leaves the present to the intrigues of the militarists.

Pacifism is haphazard: it wants to prevent war without replacing it; its negative goal lacks the positive program of an active world policy. Pacifism is splintered; it has sects, but no church; its groups work in isolation, without uniform leadership and organization.

Pacifism tends to be an appendage rather than a centerpiece of political programs; their focus is on domestic politics, while their pacifism is more a tactic than a principle.

Pacifism is inconsequential; it usually agrees to resign without criticism to a higher ideal (that is to say, a clever catchphrase)—as it did in 1914 and would be willing to do so in the future.

The biggest evil of pacifism is the pacifists. This does not change the fact that among them are the best and most important men of our time. These are excluded from the following criticism.

Most pacifists are fanatics, who despise politics and its means, instead of pursue them. Therefore, much to the detriment of their purpose, they are not taken seriously, politically.

Many pacifists believe that they can change the world by preaching rather than action: they compromise political pacifism by asserting it with religious and metaphysical speculations.

Usually the fear of war is the mother of pacifism. If this fear extends to the rest of the pacifists' lives, it prevents them from exposing themselves to the idea of peace.

Bravery and sacrifice are less common in pacifists than in militarists. Many recognize the danger of war—but few make personal or material sacrifices to avert them. Instead of fighters, they are quarrelsome pacifists, who leave others to the battle, in whose fruits they partake.

Many pacifists have gentle natures and not only shy away from war—but also from the battle against war; their heart is pure, but their will is weak and therefore their fighting value illusory.

Most pacifists are weak-minded, like most people; unable to resist mass suggestion at the decisive moment—they are pacifists during peace, militarists during the war. Only a solid organization, led by strong will, can force them into the service of peace.

3. RELIGIOUS AND POLITICAL PACIFISM

Religious pacifism fights war because it is not moral—political pacifism because it is not profitable.

Religious pacifism sees crime in a war—political pacifism sees stupidity.

Religious pacifism seeks to abolish war by changing people—political pacifism by changing situations.

Both forms of pacifism are good and justified: separately, they serve human peace and progress; merged, they harm one another more than they benefit each other. However, they should consciously support each other: so, it goes without saying that the political pacifist should also use ethical arguments to strengthen the advertising power of propaganda; and a religious pacifist should support pacifist politics instead of militaristic—if he has a choice.

In its methods, however, *practical pacifism* must emancipate itself from ethical pacifism: otherwise, it will be unable to successfully lead the fight against militarism. In politics, the Machiavellian methods of militarism have proved more effective than the Tolstoian methods of pacifism, which consequently had to surrender in 1914 and 1919. If pacifism wants to win in the future, it must learn from its opponents and pursue its goals with Machiavellian means: he has to learn from robbers how to deal with robbers. Because whoever throws his weapon away in the name of nonviolence, while being robbed, helps only the robbers, only violence, only the wrong. Therefore, the political pacifist must acknowledge the fact that in daily politics nonviolence is not equal to violence; that only he can renounce violence who, as once Christianity, can wait for centuries. But Europe cannot: if peace does not prevail here, in 300 years only Chinese archaeologists will disturb its rest in the cemetery. So, it is not enough for European peace to win: if it does not win soon, its victory is illusory.

Anyone who wants to play a game successfully, must submit to the rules of the game. *The rules of politics are: cunning and violence.*

If pacifism wants to intervene in politics, it must use these means to combat militarism. Only after its victory could it change the rules of the game and put law in place of power.

But as long as in politics power is above law, pacifism must lean on power. If he leaves power to the friends of war, while it only relies on his own rights as a matter of principle, it only advances the future wars.

A politician who does not want to use violence is like a surgeon who does not want to cut: here and there it is important to find the right measure between too much and too little: otherwise the patient dies instead of recovering.

Politics is the science of conquest and the right use of power. The inner peace of all countries is upheld by law and violence: law without violence would immediately lead to chaos and anarchy, that is, to the worst form of violence.

The same fate is threatening international peace, if its rights are not supported by an international organization of power.

Pacifism as a political program must therefore never reject violence: it must use it against the war—not for it.

The mistrust of the peace-loving masses in the political leadership of the pacifists, which seems to be paradoxical, is explained by the fact that most pacifists do not know the ABCs of politics. Because, just as we prefer to entrust our representation to a skilled lawyer rather than a clumsy one—even if he is kind, so too nations prefer to put their fate into clever hands rather than in benevolent hands.

Pacifists will only conquer the political trust of the masses if, in the words of the bible, they are not only gentle as doves but also clever as snakes; if they are not only nobler, but also more skilled in the means, than their militaristic rivals.

4. REFORM OF PACIFISM

The new era demands a new pacifism. Statesmen should be its leaders instead of dreamers; fighters should fill its ranks, instead of complainers!

Only an intelligent pacifism can convince the masses, only a heroic pacifism can sway them!

The new pacifists should be optimists of the will, but pessimists of knowledge. They should neither overlook nor exaggerate the dangers threatening peace—but fight them. The claim, "a new war is impossible" is a wrong as "a new war is inevitable". Whether or not the possibility of war will turn into the reality of war depends first and foremost on the pacifists' energy and prudence. Because war and peace are not natural events—but man made.

Therefore, the pacifist must take the following point of view: "Peace is being threatened; peace is possible; peace is desirable; let's create peace!"

The new pacifism must limit its goals in order to achieve them, and to only demand what he is determined to enforce. Because the realm of peace can only be conquered step by step and one step forward in reality is worth more than a thousand steps in the imagination.

Boundless programs only lure fantasists while repelling politicians; but a politician can do more for peace than a thousand fantasists!

The pacifists of all nations, parties and ideologies must form a phalanx in international politics with unified leadership and common symbols.

Merging so many diverse groups is impossible and inappropriate—but their cooperation is possible and necessary.

Pacifism must demand clarity from every politician about his position on war and peace. In this life question, every voter has a right to know the position of his candidate, to know under what precise circumstances he would vote for the war and what means he wants to use to prevent war.

Only if voters intervene in foreign policy in this way, instead of being content with phrases and slogans, could the parliaments become mirror images of the will that animate the masses of workers, farmers and citizens of all nations.

Above all, the new pacifism must reform the pacifists.

Pacifism can only win if the pacifists are willing to sacrifice honor, money and life; if rich pacifists pay, the strong pacifists act.

As long as the masses see heroes in the militarists who are prepared daily to give their lives for their ideals, but only weaklings and cowards in the pacifists, enthusiasm for war will be stronger than enthusiasm for peace.

Because the power to convince lies in things—the power of enthusiasm in people. The more pacifists become fighters, apostles, heroes and martyrs of their idea, rather than their advocates and beneficiaries, the stronger their power to inspire will be.

5. WORLD PEACE AND EUROPEAN PEACE

The objectives of religious pacifism are absolute and simple—the objectives of political pacifism are relative and diverse. Every political problem calls for a specific type of pacifism.

There are three main types of war: offensive war, defensive war and war of liberation.

All pacifists are opponents of the war of conquest; the way to combat it is clear: mutual commitment of states to a common defense against peace-breakers. In the future, such an organization, which the League of Nations is planning through the Guarantee Pact, will protect nations from wars of conquest and at the same time spare them individual defensive actions.

The problem of the liberation war is much more difficult. Because its form is that of an offensive war, but its soul is that of a defensive war against a conquest. Pacifism which makes wars of liberation impossible, sides with the party of the oppressors. On the other hand, an international legitimization of the liberation war would be a promise of wars of conquest.

Because the liberation of oppressed peoples and classes is the most popular excuse for all wars of conquest; and because everywhere there exist nations, races and classes who feel oppressed, or really are oppressed, today a pacifism that permits a war of liberation would be practically illusory.

Two theories are facing each other here: conservative pacifism, whose goal it is to fight every peace breaker, to preserve the status quo and the current conditions of ruling—and revolutionary pacifism whose goal is one last world war for the liberation of all oppressed classes, peoples and races and thus the destruction of any future cause for war and the creation of the world republic.

Conservative pacifism is centered in the Geneva league of Nations—revolutionary pacifism in the Moscow Treaty.

Geneva pacifism wants to maintain peace without eliminating the weapons that threaten to lead to a future war; Moscow pacifism wants to accelerate the international explosion in order to secure peace for the future.

It is to be feared that Geneva will be too weak to keep the peace—and Moscow too weak to build it. That is why both brands threaten world peace with their radicalism.

A partial way out of this dilemma is an evolutionary pacifism whose objective is a gradual erosion of national and social oppression while maintaining peace. This pacifism, which leads like a narrow rope over a double abyss, requires the highest political skill of the leaders and great political understanding by nations. Nevertheless, it must be tried by all those who honestly want peace.

The two most difficult peace problems of the future: The Indian and the Australian problem. In the Indian question, (which is a special case of the general colonial issue) the will of the Indian nation for political independence and the will of the UK to keep it in its union are seemingly irreconcilable. This situation tempts the Asian (and semi-

Asian) peoples to one day unite with India in a great war of liberation.

The Australian question (which is a special case of the Pacific immigration issue) revolves around the lockout of the Mongols from the Anglo-Saxon settlements. The strong population growth of the Mongols is not proportionate to their lack of settlement areas and threatens to one day cause an explosion in the Pacific Ocean, if a valve is not opened. On the other hand, the white Australians know that admittance of the Mongols would soon push them into a minority. Which solution finds this problem, once China is as armed as Japan, is unclear.

The peaceful solution to these world problems is a very difficult task for the British, Asian and Australian pacifists.

However, European pacifists must clearly recognize that a violent solution to these questions is more likely than a peaceful one—but that they lack the power and the influence to prevent these threatening wars.

This insight clarifies the mission of European pacifism: he does not have the power to pacify the globe—but it does have the power to give permanent peace to Europe by solving the European question and by preventing his part of the earth from getting involved in the Asian and Pacific conflicts. As a result, Europe's political pacifism must limit its objectives and learn to distinguish between what it wants—and what it can achieve. Without overstretching its powers, it must first fight for peace in his own part of the world and leave it to the Americans, Brits, Russians and Asians to keep the peace in the parts of the world that have fallen to them. But all pacifists around the world must stay in constant contact with each other, as many problems (especially disarmament) are to be solved internationally, and since international pacifism must try to avoid and settle conflicts between those world complexes.

Compared to those East Asian war threats, European peace issues are relatively easy to solve. No insurmountable obstacle stands in the way of European peace. Nobody could win anything in a European war, but everyone could lose everything. The victor would be mortally wounded—the defeated would emerge destroyed from this mass murder.

Therefore, a new European war could only arise from a crime by the militarists, through carelessness of the pacifists and stupidity of politicians.

It can be prevented if the warmongers are kept in check in every country, if pacifists fulfill their duty and the statesmen safeguard the interests of their peoples.

The securing of peace in Europe, which has become the Balkan of the world, represents a significant step forward towards world peace. Just as the World War emanated from Europe—world peace might emanate from Europe.

There is no way of thinking about world peace unless European peace is anchored in a stable system.

6. REALPOLITIK PEACE PROGRAM

The European threat of war is divided into two groups: the first is founded on national oppression—the second in social oppression. Today, the border issue and the Russian question threaten European peace.

The essence of the border issue is that most European states and peoples are dissatisfied with their current borders, because they do not meet the national, economic or strategic demands of the Nationalists. A peaceful change of today's borders is impossible: therefore, the nationalists of those dissatisfied states are preparing for violent change of the borders by a new war, forcing their neighbors to arm themselves.

The Russian question is rooted in the fact that there is a world power on the open border with Europe, whose leaders' goal it is to violently overthrow the existing European system. In order to achieve this goal, they support the social irredenta of Europe with money and hope to follow up with Soviet troops after the outbreak of a European revolution.

For reasons of principle, Russia is opposing modern-day pacifism, is committed to militaristic methods and organizing a strong army to use it to change the world map—at least in Europe and Asia. Once this army is strong enough, it will undoubtedly march against the west.

These two problems, which occur at individual points (Bessarabia, Eastern Galicia), threaten the peace of Europe on a daily basis. Every European pacifist must deal with them and try to avert them.

The "Pan-Europa Program" is the only way to prevent these two threats with real political means and to ensure European peace.

Its goal is:

1. Securing inner-European peace through a pan-European arbitration agreement, guarantee pact, customs union and minority protection.
2. Securing peace with Russia through a pan-European alliance, through mutual recognition, non-interference and border guarantee, joint disarmament and economic cooperation, as well as by reducing social oppression.
3. Securing peace with Britain, America and East Asia through arbitration agreements and regional reform of the League of Nations

The Pan-Europa Program is the only possible solution to the European border problem. The incompatibility of all national aspirations, as well as the tension between geographic-strategic, historical-economic and national borders in Europe makes a fair border management impossible. A change of the borders would eliminate old injustices, but put new ones in their place.

Therefore, a solution of the European border problem is only possible by turning it off.

The two elements of the solution are:

A. The conservative element of territorial status quo, which stabilizes the existing borders and thus prevents an impending war.

B. The revolutionary element of gradual elimination of borders in strategic, economic and national ways that destroy the possibility of future wars.

This securing of the borders, combined with their dismantling, preserves the formal organization of Europe, while changing the west.

In this way it secures the present and future peace, as well as the economic and national development of Europe.

The other European danger of war is the Russian one. On the one hand, Russian militarization springs from fear of an anti-Bolshevik invasion supported by Europe—on the other, the will to launch an aggressive war against Europe in the name of social liberation.

Therefore, it must be the aim of European pacifism to secure both Russia from a European and Europe from a Russian attack. The first is only possible through a will of peace—the second through military superiority. This military superiority can be immediately achieved by Europe without increasing its armaments through a pan-European defense alliance.

European pacifism must not allow this superiority to degenerate into an arms race, but must make it the basis of Russian-European disarmament and understanding.

Europe does not have the possibility to change the political stance of the Russian rulers, whose system is expansive. Since it cannot persuade them of peace, it must force them into peace. If one neighbor is peaceful, the other warlike, pacifism demands that military superiority be on the side of peace. A reversal of this relationship means war.

It is a delusion of many pacifists to see the safe way to peace in their own disarmament. Under certain circumstances, peace demands disarmament—but in other circumstances, armament. For example, if England and Belgium had strong armies in 1914, the British mediation proposal would have been more likely to be accepted shortly before the catastrophe.

If, for example, a pacifist nation refuses to join the war while their neighbors lurk on the opportunity to invade it, it does not promote peace, but war.

If another nation increases its weapons to secure its peace and thereby provokes a peaceful neighbor to an arms race, it does not promote peace but war.

Every peace problem demands an individual action. Therefore, Europe cannot apply the same methods for peace with England and Russia.

Peace with England, whose policy is stable and pacifist, can be based on treaties—peace with Russia, which is in a revolution and does not deny its war plans against the European system, needs military security.

It would be equally unpolitical and un-pacifistic to rely on agreements with the Soviets, as towards England on the fleet. On the other hand, European pacifism must always be prepared, to face a pacifist Russia, which has disarmed and honestly renounced its plans for invasion the same way as a pacifist England.

But European pacifists must never forget that Russia is arming itself in the name of social liberation and that millions of Europeans would regard a Russian invasion as a war of liberation. This war becomes all the more threatening the more this conviction spreads throughout the masses of Europe.

Just as the national threats of war can only be averted by breaking down national oppression, this social danger of war can only be averted by breaking down social oppression.

The social irredenta of Europe will only drop out of the Moscow Treaty if it is provided with practical proof that the situation and future of workers in the democratic countries is better than in the Soviet. If communism can prove the opposite, no foreign policy can save Europe from the revolution and the union with Soviet Russia.

This shows the close connection between domestic and foreign policy—freedom and peace. As any oppression, whether it is national or social, carries with it the seeds of war, the fight against oppression forms an integral part of the fight for peace.

Every oppression forces the oppressors to maintain military power, and the oppressed and their allies to warmongering. Conversely, a war and armament policy provide state rulers with the strongest instrument for domestic oppression: the army. Therefore, the peace of Europe and the world will only be permanently secured when religions, nations and classes cease feeling oppressed.

That is why peaceful foreign policy goes hand in hand with liberal domestic policy—but foreign war policy with oppression inside.

7. PROMOTING THE IDEA OF PEACE

In addition to fighting for its foreign policy peace program, the pacifist should not miss the opportunity to promote international cooperation and understanding.

This determines the attitude of pacifism to the League of Nations.

Today's League of Nations is very imperfect as a peace institution; above all, it is heavily burdened by the inheritance of the war that gave birth to it. It is weak, unarticulated, unreliable; it is unfinished as long as the United States, Germany and Russia are absent from it. Nevertheless, the Geneva League of Nations is the first draft of an international world organization that is to replace the current anarchy of the nations.

It has this immense advantage over all better institutions, which are only projects.

Therefore, every pacifist must support the weak, frail, embryonic League of Nations; he should criticize it, but not fight it; work on its transformation, but not on its destruction.

Every pacifist should help eliminate the stupid hatred between nations, which harms everyone and does no good. He can do this best by spreading the truth and combating malicious and uneducated hate speech.

One of the main causes of national hatred is that nations do not know each other and, seeing only the statements of a chauvinist press and literature, perceive them only in distorted images. In order to fight these attitudes, pacifism should create an enlightened literature, promote translations, as well as the exchange of professors, teachers, students and children. An international agreement should aim to combat chauvinist hate speech against foreign nations in schools and the press.

In order to promote the idea of peace and to combat war, peace ministries should be established in all nations, which, in constant contact with each other and with all the pacifist organizations at home and abroad, serve international reconciliation.

One of the most important tasks of pacifism is the introduction of a common language. Because before the nations can talk to each other, it is difficult to expect them to understand each other.

An international common language would have the purpose that every person speaks their native language at home, while using the common language in dealing with foreign nationals. Every person who leaves his homeland needs only one common language, whereas today he needs several languages abroad. As a common language, only Esperanto and English come into question. Which of these is chosen is irrelevant as long as the world agrees on one of these two.

The English language has the great advantage over Esperanto that it has already assumed the role of an international common language in half of Asia, Africa and America, as well as large parts of Europe, so that in these areas their official introduction would only be the sanctioning of existing practice. In its intermediate position between Germanic and Roman languages it is easily learnable for Germans as well as for Romans, as well as for Slavs, who already speak a Germanic or Roman language. In addition, English is the language of the two most powerful parts of the earth and the most widely used native language of white mankind.

The introduction of the international common language could be made through a proposal by the League of Nations to enforce it in all middle schools and teacher training centers in the world, and after a decade also in primary schools.

The spreading of enlightenment and the fight against human ignorance have faster chances of success for peace propaganda than the spreading of charity and the fight against evil.

Because human beliefs change faster than human instincts, and at least in Europe, the peace movement would have no need to appeal to the human heart—if it could rely on the human mind.

Just as enlightenment ended witch-burning, torture and slavery—so will it someday end war, the remnant of a barbaric age of mankind.

When this will happen is unknown; that it will happen is certain. It depends on the pacifists. That humans finally learned to fly after hundreds of thousands of years was much more wonderful and unlikely than one day learning to live in peace with one another.

8. PEACE PROPAGANDA

Peace propaganda is the necessary complement to peace policy: because pacifist policy is short term—pacifist propaganda long term.

Peace propaganda alone is incapable of preventing the imminent threat of war, since it requires at least two generations for its impact; peace policy alone is incapable of securing permanent peace, as the rapid development of our age barely extends the sphere of influence of politics over two generations.

At best, peace policy can, with great skill, create a temporary arrangement to give peace propaganda the opportunity to morally disarm the nations, and to convince them that war is a barbaric, impractical, and outmoded means of dealing with international differences.

For, as long as this knowledge has not prevailed internationally and as long as there are nations who regard war as the most appropriate means of accomplishing their political goals, peace cannot be based on disarmament, but only on the military superiority of the pacifists.

Complete disarmament is only possible after the victory of the peace idea—the abolition of the police would be possible after the extinction of criminality: otherwise the abolition of the police leads to a dictatorship of crime—the abolition of the army to a dictatorship of war.

Pacifist propaganda is directed against war instincts, war interests and ideals of war. The fight against war instincts must be led by their weakening and by distraction as well as by strengthening of opposing instincts.

Above all, it is important to wean war nations and thus let their war instincts die off, like smokers, alcoholics and morphine addicts losing their addictions by not using. The means for the cessation of war is peace policy.

Sport is very suitable to distract human—especially male fighting instincts from the attraction of war. It is no coincidence that the most sports-loving nations of Europe (England, Scandinavia) are also the most peaceful.

Only hunting is an exception here: it preserves the most primitive form of combat and strengthens the instinct to kill, rather than divert it. It has done much to preserve European militarism, since hunting was the main sport of the ruling classes and rulers; because hunting incites disrespect for life and desensitizes against bloodshed.

Condemnation of war must never degenerate into condemnation of fighting. Such derailment of pacifism would only play into the hands of the militarists, ethically and biologically compromising pacifism.

Because fighting and the will to fight are creators and preservers of human culture.

The end of fighting and the death of human fighting instincts would be synonymous with the end and death of culture and of man.

Fighting is good; only war is bad, because it is a primitive, crude and obsolete form of international battle, as duels are a primitive, crude and obsolete form of social battle.

The goal of pacifism is not the abolition of combat, but the refinement, sublimation and modernization of its methods.

Nowadays, economic combat is about to replace the armed combat: boycott and blockade are replacing war, and the political protest has replaced the revolution. China has won several political battles against Japan with boycotts, and Gandhi is trying to win the Indian liberation war in this bloodless way.

A time will come when national rivalry will be fought with weapons of the mind, instead of knives and bullets. Instead of arms races, nations will compete with each other in scientific, artistic and technological achievements, in justice and social welfare, in public health and public education and in bringing forth great personalities.

The second task of peace propaganda is the fight against war interests. This propaganda is to show nations and individuals the low chances of profit and the tremendous risk of losses, with the result of war becoming a bad, risky and unprofitable business.

As far as nations are concerned, Norman Angell already proved this before the war, and the world war has confirmed his thesis brilliantly.

Whether, from a national point of view a victorious liberation war in India or a conquest of Australia by the Mongols would outweigh the victims may remain unexplained here; but it is certain that in a new European war the winner would emerge severely damaged politically, economically and nationally, while the defeated nation would be destroyed forever. The potential profit is in no way relative to the losses.

Interested in war are only ambitious politicians and military who hope for glory on the one hand, and greedy war suppliers who hope for business, on the other. These groups are very small, but very powerful.

The first group can be cooled by a determined pacifism in democratic states: politicians who place their ambitions above the wellbeing of their nation shall be treated like criminals.

It is often said about officers, that their war ambitions are their professional duty. In pacifist nations, this would be a flaw, because there the army is not a means of conquest, but as a necessary weapon against foreign will of war. It would therefore be necessary for the officers to be educated as pacifists, but heroic pacifists who are always prepared to sacrifice their lives to the maintenance of peace and who see themselves as crusaders in the fight against war.

The industrialists, who long for war for the profits, should be reminded that at the end of the next European war is Bolshevism. They can expect expropriation, if not the gallows. The war business loses its appeal through this prospect. For it seems more advantageous for industry to be content with relatively narrow but safe peace gains, instead of reaching for the fat but life-threatening war profits.

These arguments are important because they remove the golden engine from war propaganda and give it to the peace propaganda.

Peace propaganda must also mobilize human imagination against a future war. It has to educate the masses about the dangers and horrors that threaten them in case of a war: about the new rays and gasses that can kill entire cities, about the threat of an extermination war, which would be directed less to the front, but to the rural areas; about the political and economic consequences of such a war for victors and defeated.

This propaganda must help weak human memory and weak human imagination: for if people had more imagination—there would be no more war. The will to live would be the strongest ally of pacifism.

War instincts are crude and primitive—war interests are problematic and dangerous—the ideals of war are false and outdated.

They falsely equate war with fighting, warriors with heroes, unimaginativeness with bravery, fear with cowardice.

They are from a lost epoch, from conditions that have been overcome. They were once shaped by a war caste and adopted by free nations without criticism.

Once, the warrior was the guardian of culture, the war hero was a true hero, war was a vital element of the nations whose fate was decided by their bravery in the field.

Since then, war has become unchivalrous, its methods vile, its forms ugly; personal bravery is no longer crucial: the miserable ugliness of a mass slaughterhouse has taken the place of the knightly beauty of a mass tournament. Today's mechanized war has forever lost its romance.

From an ethical point of view, a defensive war is organized self-defense—an offensive war is organized murder. Worse still: peaceful people are being forced to poison and tear other peaceful people to pieces. Worse still: peaceful people are being brutally forced to poison and tear other peaceful people to pieces.

The blame for this instigated mass murder does not fall on the executors, but on the instigators. In democratic states these instigators are the pro-war parliamentarians, and indirectly their voters. Therefore, anyone who is afraid to commit murder should think twice about whom he sends to parliament.

9. NEW HEROISM

The renewal of the hero ideal through pacifism shatters the main weapon of militarist propaganda. For nothing gives militarism greater power than a monopoly on heroism.

Pacifism would commit suicide by fighting the heroic ideal; he would lose all his valuable followers—for the reverence for heroism is the measure of human nobleness.

The knowledge that the heroism of Christ is a higher form of evolution than the heroism of Achilles must penetrate—and that the physical heroes of the past are only the precursors of the moral hero of the future.

No honest pacifist would try to kill the heroism of men who have put their lives on the line for their ideals beyond mandatory military service; who have voluntarily set aside their family's happiness, their comfort, safety and health to fulfill their duty. Their heroism is not affected by the question of whether it originated from false or correct assumptions. Nothing would be meaner than the mockery of this type of heroism.

The opposite of those heroes are the demagogues who promote war in assemblies, editorial offices, and parliaments, and then, far from the front make use of such heroism.

The attempt by some militarists to monopolize heroism for the war party is just as dishonest as the attempt by some nationalists to monopolize the national spirit.

Because whoever wants to preserve his people from the greatest catastrophe in world history is at least as patriotic as the one who hopes for new power through a victorious war; the former is building on error, the latter on truth.

Today, there are some European countries where it is more life-threatening to fight for peace than for war: in these countries, pacifists prove a greater heroic courage than war mongers.

The most serious and unjust insult to a nation is when a rank, such as the rank of officer, monopolizes the heroic character: because there is heroism in every profession, quiet and great heroism, without fame, without romance and without a glittering façade; the heroism of work and mind, the heroism of motherhood, the heroism of conviction.

And whoever studies the biographies of great artists, thinkers, researchers, inventors and physicians, will understand that there is heroism other than that of warriors and adventurers.

Everyone is a hero who sacrifices his own interest for his ideal: the greater the sacrifice, the greater the heroism.

He who is not afraid, is not heroic, but unimaginative. Only he acts heroically, who overcomes his fear for the sake of his ideal: the greater the fear, the greater his overcoming and heroism.

Europe has freed itself from the rule of feudalism—but not from the rule of feudal values. As a result, the heroic ideal has become just as untimely and rotten as the concept of honor. Only a renewal can save it.

The honor of a human being and of a nation should be determined independent from foreign action and be determined solely by their own actions.

The principal must prevail that the honor of a nation can never be violated by its flag being lowered by drunks somewhere, but only by the fact that its judges are partisan, their officials can be bribed and their statesmen don't keep their word; that it banishes or murders its best sons, provokes weaker neighbors, oppresses minorities, neglects its obligations and breaks its agreements.

Through this new code of honor, all the quarrels that divide nations and drive them to wars will naturally cease: for every nation will then consider it their honor to do something for others—not to honor them, but to preserve or restore their own national honor. Satisfaction of this code can then easily be determined by arbitration.

Pacifism must educate present and future educations in the *heroism of conviction*. Lies and cowardice were to blame for the outbreak of the war; they nourished and sustained it, and finally put their stamp on peace as well. That is why the fight against lies is also a fight against war. Heroism of peace becomes heroism of the mind, of conviction, self-control; only then can it triumph over the heroism of the militarists.

This heroism of peace is more difficult and rarer than that of war. It is harder to direct one's passions than one's team, harder to discipline one's own character than an army of recruits. And many who could easily run a bayonet into the body of a foe, do not find the courage to admit their convictions to a friend. This moral cowardice is the soil for all demagogy, including the militaristic: out of fear of appearing cowardly, millions today deny their inner pacifism, preferring to be cowardly rather than appear cowardly.

The victory of the peace idea is intimately related to the triumph of moral heroism, which is willing to sacrifice everything but its conviction, and to keep itself pure against all attempts of persuasion, extortion and bribery in an impure time.

Such peace heroes should be organized into a voluntary peace army in all European nations.

This army of peace should be recruited from heroes who reject war as a barbaric and nonsensical means of politics and as an enemy of humanity, and who are always prepared to sacrifice for their pacifist beliefs.

First, these warriors of peace should be propagandists and agitators who spread their ideas to the millions who want peace. But the peace army must be also ready to match at the crucial moment against the war, and to save peace through its active intervention.

At the forefront of this army should be men who combine a statesmanlike insight with unbending and unwavering will for peace.

Only if such leaders are at the head of such fighters, Europe can hope to never be overrun and pounded by war again.

Other publications

OMNIA VERITAS
Omnia Veritas Ltd presents:
THE WORLD ORDER
OUR SECRET RULERS
A Study in the Hegemony of Parasitism
by
EUSTACE MULLINS
The peoples of the world not only will never love Big Brother, but they will soon dispose of him forever.
The program of the World Order remains the same; Divide and Conquer

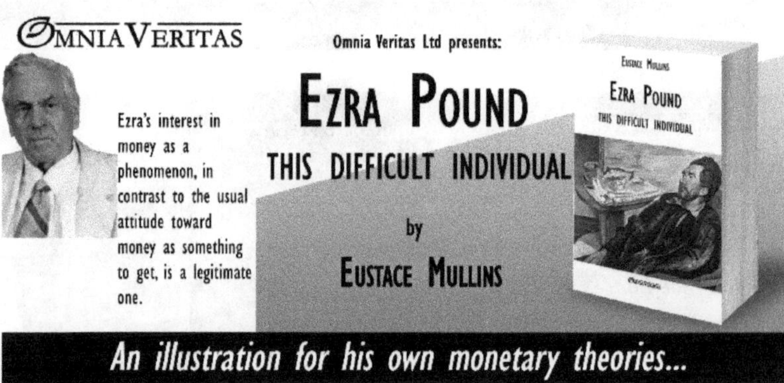
OMNIA VERITAS
Omnia Veritas Ltd presents:
EZRA POUND
THIS DIFFICULT INDIVIDUAL
by
EUSTACE MULLINS
Ezra's interest in money as a phenomenon, in contrast to the usual attitude toward money as something to get, is a legitimate one.
An illustration for his own monetary theories...

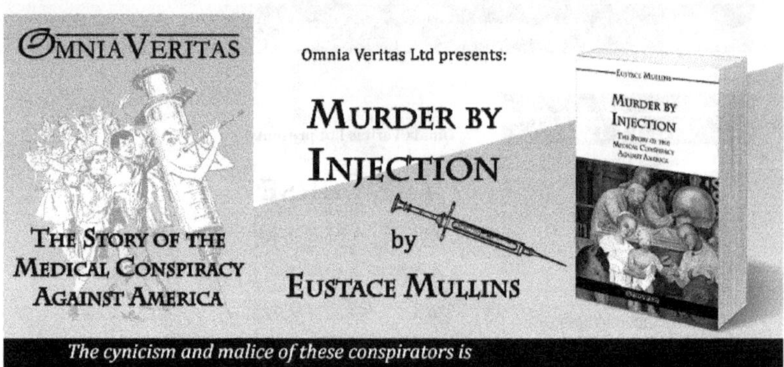
OMNIA VERITAS
Omnia Veritas Ltd presents:
MURDER BY INJECTION
by
EUSTACE MULLINS
THE STORY OF THE MEDICAL CONSPIRACY AGAINST AMERICA
The cynicism and malice of these conspirators is something beyond the imagination of most Americans.

OMNIA VERITAS
OMNIA VERITAS LTD PRESENTS:
MY LIFE IN
CHRIST
BY
EUSTACE MULLINS
Christ did not wish to be followed by robots and sleepwalkers, He desired man to awaken, and to attain the full use of his earthly powers.
THIS is the story of my life in Christ

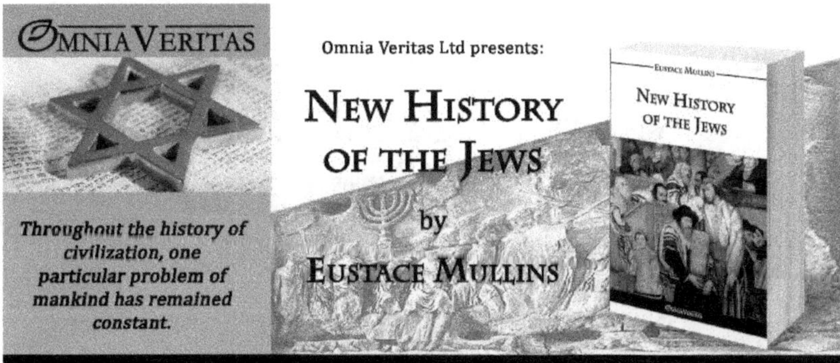
OMNIA VERITAS
Omnia Veritas Ltd presents:
NEW HISTORY
OF THE JEWS
by
EUSTACE MULLINS
Throughout the history of civilization, one particular problem of mankind has remained constant.
Only one people bas irritated its host nations in every part of the civilized world

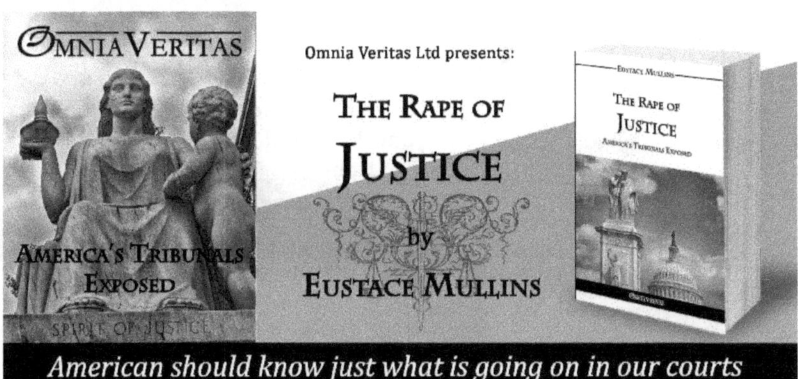
OMNIA VERITAS
Omnia Veritas Ltd presents:
THE RAPE OF
JUSTICE
by
EUSTACE MULLINS
AMERICA'S TRIBUNALS EXPOSED
SPIRIT OF JUSTICE
American should know just what is going on in our courts

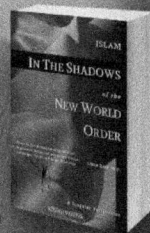

OMNIA VERITAS
The meaning of Monarchy's struggle against the Money Power
Omnia Veritas Ltd presents:
Monarchy or Money POWER
by
ROBERT MCNAIR WILSON
A master-piece of history
The true nature of Kingship revealed!

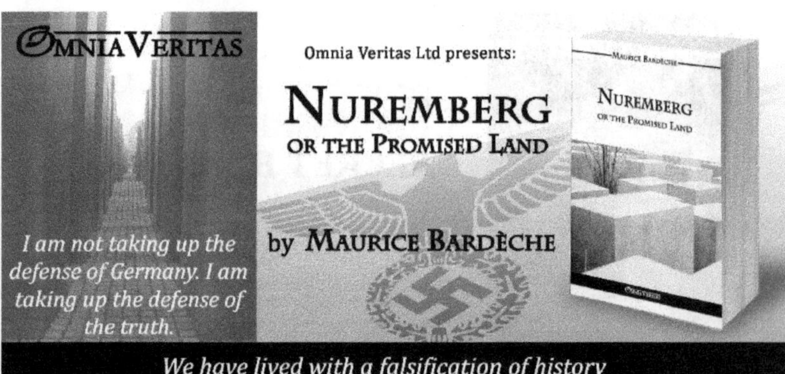
OMNIA VERITAS
Omnia Veritas Ltd presents:
NUREMBERG
OR THE PROMISED LAND
by MAURICE BARDÈCHE
I am not taking up the defense of Germany. I am taking up the defense of the truth.
We have lived with a falsification of history

OMNIA VERITAS
Omnia Veritas Ltd presents:
Practical Suggestions for Mother and Housewife
by MARION MILLS MILLER
The mother or matron was named from the most tender and sacred of human functions
What tender associations halo the names of wife, mother, sister and daughter!

The time has come for a ***book*** *like this to command the attention of* ***medical*** *men...*

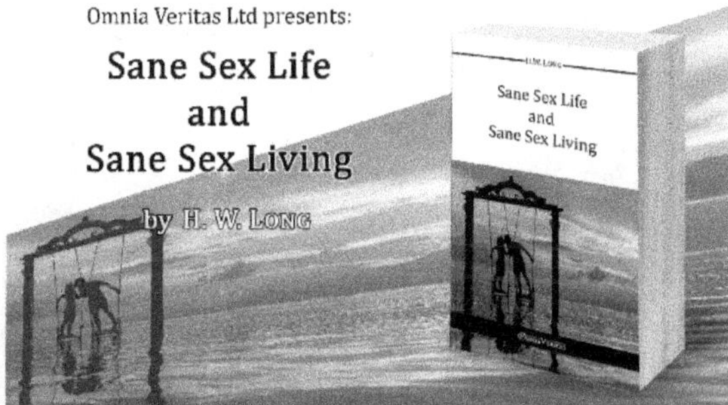

... they never learned sex. They never realized its fundamentals...

Omnia Veritas Ltd presents:

SVALI SPEAKS

BREAKING FREE OF CULT PROGRAMMING

UNDERSTAND ILLUMINATI CULT PROGRAMMING

Modern day Illuminism is a philosophy funded by the wealthy

OMNIA VERITAS
"There was a class of persons who very well understood each other's interests, who very likely were related by racial and religious custom, and whose supra-nationalism transcended all city boundaries and borders of states."
Omnia Veritas Ltd presents:
The Babylonian Woe
by
DAVID ASTLE
"Yesterday it was a conspiracy against the men of a city, or a relatively small state; today a conspiracy against the whole world."
The Babylonian Woe
David Astle's masterpiece in a brand new edition!

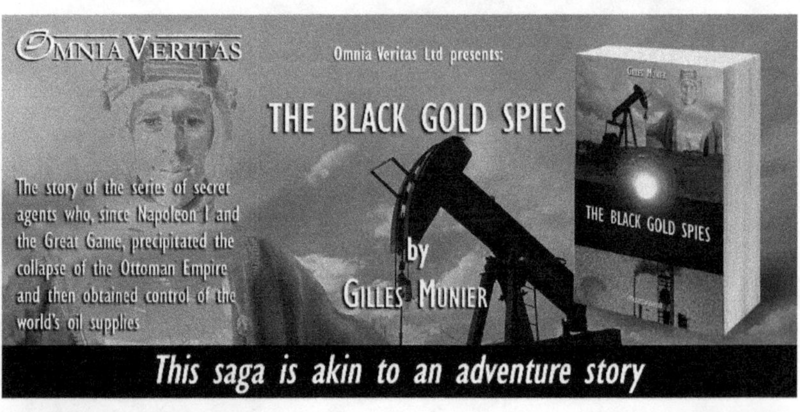
OMNIA VERITAS
Omnia Veritas Ltd presents:
THE BLACK GOLD SPIES
The story of the series of secret agents who, since Napoleon I and the Great Game, precipitated the collapse of the Ottoman Empire and then obtained control of the world's oil supplies
by
GILLES MUNIER
THE BLACK GOLD SPIES
This saga is akin to an adventure story

OMNIA VERITAS
Omnia Veritas Ltd presents :
THE CONTROVERSY OF ZION
by
Douglas Reed
Douglas Reed's book is the missing link unveiling the multisecular plot.
Zionism:
Centuries of Struggle to reclaim the Holy Land
THE CONTROVERSY OF ZION
Resurrected true history !

OMNIA VERITAS
Historians are finding less and less to celebrate about the Revolution...
Omnia Veritas Ltd presents:
THE FRENCH Revolution
A Study in Democracy
by
NESTA WEBSTER
An account of the bloody terror, the mob violence, and the overthrow of French religious tradition...
Hard political and historical facts compiled in this essential classic!

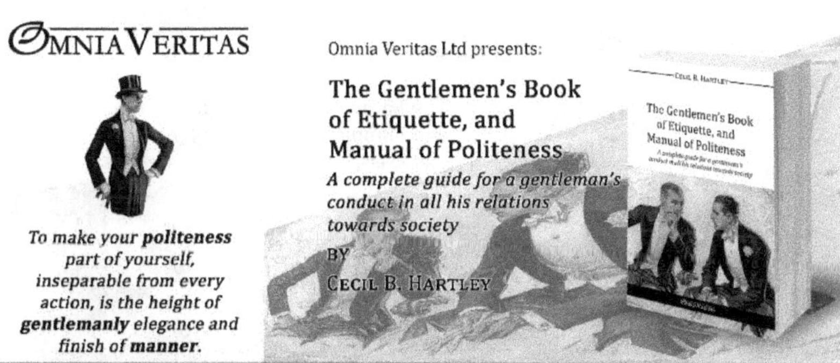
OMNIA VERITAS
Omnia Veritas Ltd presents:
The Gentlemen's Book of Etiquette, and Manual of Politeness
A complete guide for a gentleman's conduct in all his relations towards society
BY
CECIL B. HARTLEY
To make your politeness part of yourself, inseparable from every action, is the height of gentlemanly elegance and finish of manner.
As you treat the world, so the world will treat you

OMNIA VERITAS
Omnia Veritas Ltd presents:
THE HIGH COST OF VENGEANCE
BY FREDA UTLEY
France and Britain refused to listen to the statesmen who said that you can have peace or vengeance, not both...
The victors refused even to discuss the terms of peace with the vanquished

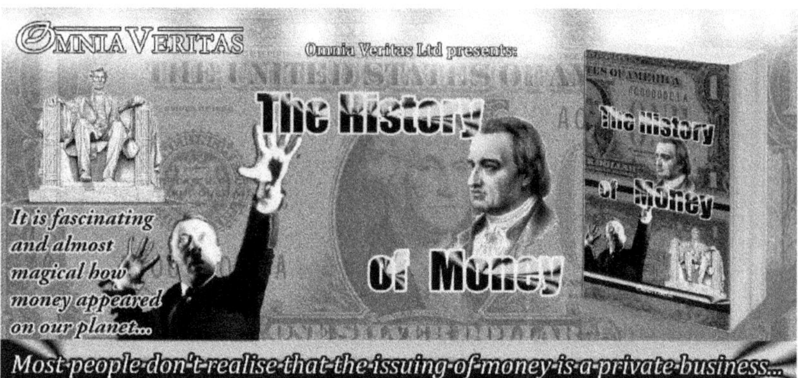
OMNIA VERITAS
Omnia Veritas Ltd presents:
The History of Money
It is fascinating and almost magical how money appeared on our planet...
Most people don't realise that the issuing of money is a private business...

OMNIA VERITAS
Omnia Veritas Ltd presents:
The Ladies' Book of Etiquette, and Manual of Politeness
A complete hand book for the use of the lady in polite society
BY
FLORENCE HARTLEY
... to be truly a lady, one must carry the principles into every circumstance of life
Politeness is goodness of heart put into daily practice

OMNIA VERITAS
A free press is the guardian genius of a just, honest, and humane democracy, as Lincoln put it:
"To sin by silence when they know they should protest, makes cowards of men."
Omnia Veritas Ltd presents:
THE LEGALIZED CRIME OF BANKING
by
SILAS WALTER ADAMS
"There is a great deal of difference between a moral wrong and a legal right"
A liberating and much acclaimed book on the Federal Reserve system!

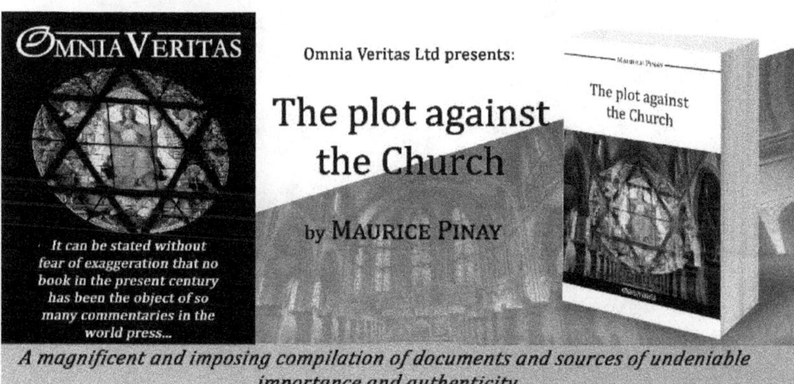

Omnia Veritas Ltd presents:

THE RIDDLE OF THE JEW'S SUCCESS

by

THEODOR FRITSCH

the Jews, however, in spite of their dispersion amongst the nations...

... still feel that they are a special people and a special race

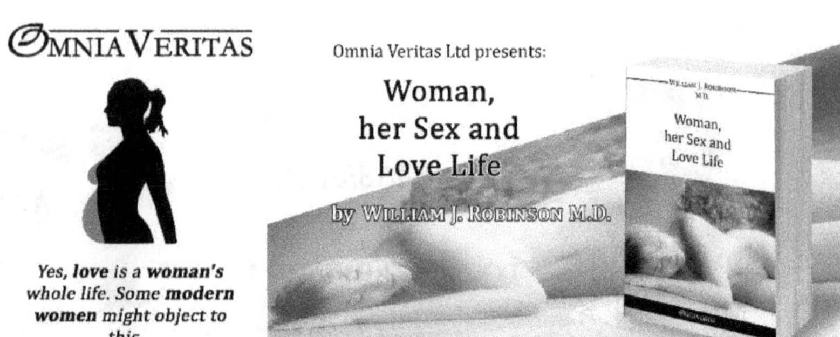
OMNIA VERITAS
Omnia Veritas Ltd presents:
Woman, her Sex and Love Life
by WILLIAM J. ROBINSON M.D.
Yes, love is a woman's whole life. Some modern women might object to this...
they will tell you if you enjoy their confidence that they are unhappy...

OMNIA VERITAS
Omnia Veritas Ltd presents:
MYRON FAGAN
THE ILLUMINATI AND THE COUNCIL ON FOREIGN RELATIONS
The objective is to brainwash the people into accepting the phony peace bait to transform the United States into an enslaved unit of the United Nations' one-world government.
They have seized that power on orders from their masters of the great conspiracy

OMNIA VERITAS
OMNIA VERITAS LTD PRESENTS
THE DISPOSSESSED MAJORITY
THE TRAGIC AND HUMILIATING FATE OF THE AMERICAN MAJORITY

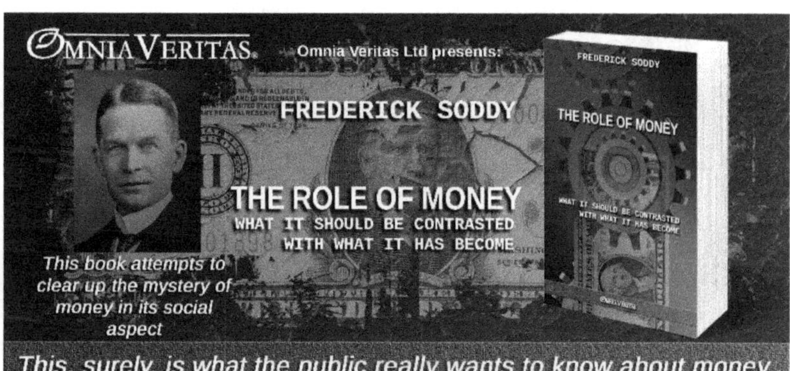
OMNIA VERITAS
Omnia Veritas Ltd presents:
FREDERICK SODDY
THE ROLE OF MONEY
WHAT IT SHOULD BE CONTRASTED
WITH WHAT IT HAS BECOME
This book attempts to clear up the mystery of money in its social aspect
This, surely, is what the public really wants to know about money

OMNIA VERITAS
Omnia Veritas Ltd presents:
FREDERICK SODDY
WEALTH, VIRTUAL WEALTH AND DEBT
THE SOLUTION OF THE ECONOMIC PARADOX
The most powerful tyranny and the most universal conspiracy against the economic freedom of individuals and the autonomy of nations the world has yet known.
The public are most carefully shielded from any real knowledge...

OMNIA VERITAS
Omnia Veritas Ltd presents:
HERVÉ RYSSEN
History of anti-Semitism set straight by a goy
The history of Judaism is the history of a people - or a sect - at permanent war against the rest of humanity...
After reading this book, we hope that no one will speak of "Judeo-Christian" civilisation any more...

OMNIA VERITAS
Omnia Veritas Ltd presents:
HERVÉ RYSSEN
ISRAEL'S BILLIONS
Since time immemorial, spread in all countries, they are famous for having dedicated themselves to the great international trade. They are also, for centuries, the masters of banking and speculation.
HERVÉ RYSSEN
ISRAEL'S BILLIONS
Jews have a very particular relationship with money...

OMNIA VERITAS
Omnia Veritas Ltd presents:
HERVÉ RYSSEN
PLANETARIAN HOPES
The triumph of democracy over communism seemed to have opened the door to a new era, to a "New World Order", and to prepare all nations for an inevitable planetary merger.
HERVÉ RYSSEN
PLANETARIAN HOPES
The idea of a world without borders and of a finally unified humanity is certainly not new...

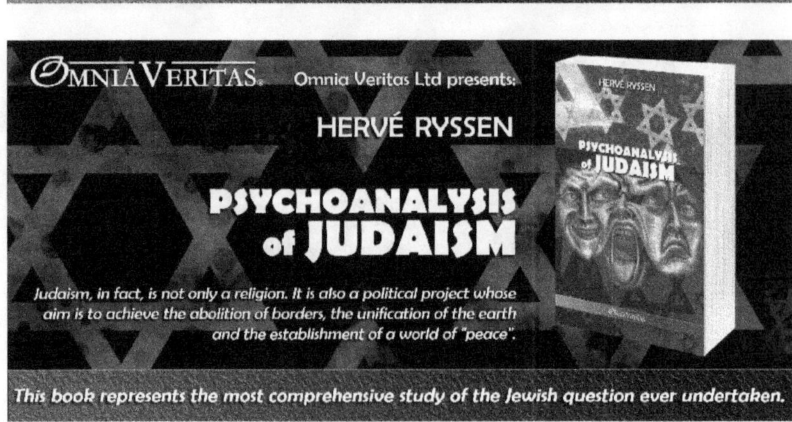
OMNIA VERITAS
Omnia Veritas Ltd presents:
HERVÉ RYSSEN
PSYCHOANALYSIS of JUDAISM
Judaism, in fact, is not only a religion. It is also a political project whose aim is to achieve the abolition of borders, the unification of the earth and the establishment of a world of "peace".
HERVÉ RYSSEN
PSYCHOANALYSIS of JUDAISM
This book represents the most comprehensive study of the Jewish question ever undertaken.

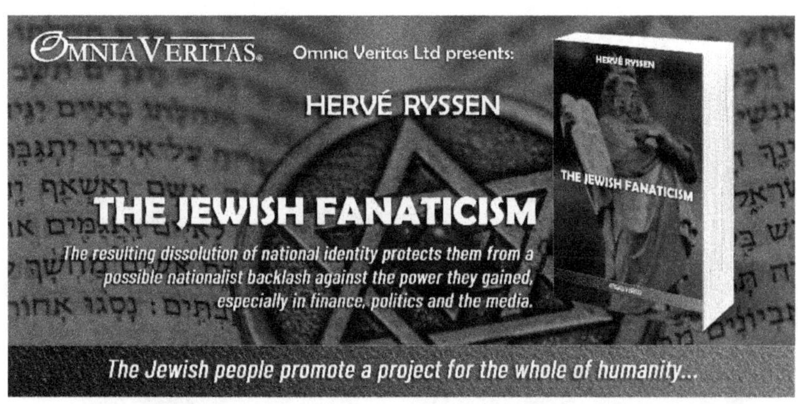
OMNIA VERITAS
Omnia Veritas Ltd presents:
HERVÉ RYSSEN
THE JEWISH FANATICISM
The resulting dissolution of national identity protects them from a possible nationalist backlash against the power they gained, especially in finance, politics and the media.
The Jewish people promote a project for the whole of humanity...

OMNIA VERITAS
Omnia Veritas Ltd presents:
HERVÉ RYSSEN
The Jewish mafia is, however, undoubtedly the most powerful mafia in the world. The most dangerous, too. Some overly curious journalists have already been killed.
The Jewish Mafia
The "Jewish mafia", that one, does not exist; the Western media do not talk about it...

OMNIA VERITAS
MK ULTRA
Ritual Abuse and Mind Control
Tools of domination for the nameless religion
For the first time, a book attempts to explore the complex subjects of traumatic ritual abuse and the mind control that results from it...
How is it possible to mentally program a human being?

OMNIA VERITAS
Omnia Veritas Ltd presents:
THE SVALI CHRONICLES
BREAKING FREE FROM MIND CONTROL
TESTIMONY OF AN EX-ILLUMINATI
The Illuminati are a group of people who follow a philosophy known as "illuminism" or "enlightenment".
THE SVALI CHRONICLES
Understanding the programming of the Illuminati sect

OMNIA VERITAS
Omnia Veritas Ltd presents:
EDWIGE THIBAUT
THE SS ORDER
ETHICS & IDEOLOGY
THE SS ORDER
ETHICS & IDEOLOGY
by EDWIGE THIBAUT
The most extraordinary political-military formation that humanity has ever known

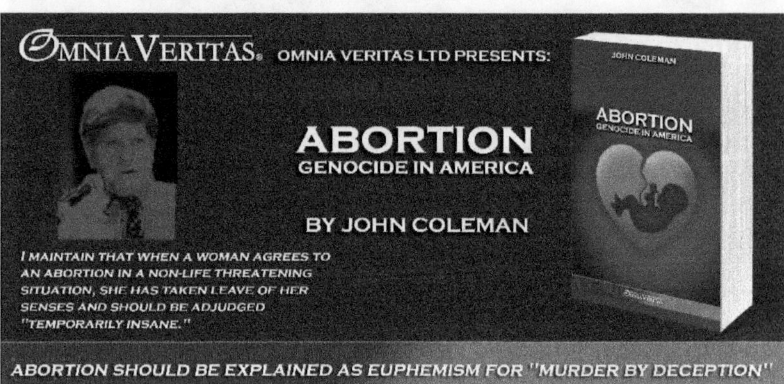
OMNIA VERITAS
OMNIA VERITAS LTD PRESENTS:
JOHN COLEMAN
ABORTION
GENOCIDE IN AMERICA
ABORTION
GENOCIDE IN AMERICA
BY JOHN COLEMAN
I MAINTAIN THAT WHEN A WOMAN AGREES TO AN ABORTION IN A NON-LIFE THREATENING SITUATION, SHE HAS TAKEN LEAVE OF HER SENSES AND SHOULD BE ADJUDGED "TEMPORARILY INSANE."
ABORTION SHOULD BE EXPLAINED AS EUPHEMISM FOR "MURDER BY DECEPTION"

OMNIA VERITAS
OMNIA VERITAS LTD PRESENTS:
BEYOND the CONSPIRACY
UNMASKING THE INVISIBLE WORLD GOVERNMENT
by John Coleman
All great historical events are planned in secret by men who surround themselves with total discretion.
Highly organized groups always have the advantage over citizens
JOHN COLEMAN
BEYOND the CONSPIRACY

OMNIA VERITAS
OMNIA VERITAS LTD PRESENTS:
THE CLUB OF ROME
THE THINK TANK OF THE NEW WORLD ORDER
BY JOHN COLEMAN
The many tragic and explosive events of the 20th century didn't happen by themselves, but were planned according to a well-established pattern...
Who were the planners and creators of these major events?
JOHN COLEMAN
THE CLUB OF ROME

OMNIA VERITAS
OMNIA VERITAS LTD PRESENTS:
DIPLOMACY BY DECEPTION
AN ACCOUNT OF THE TREASONOUS CONDUCT BY THE GOVERNMENTS OF BRITAIN AND THE UNITED STATES
BY JOHN COLEMAN
The story of the creation of the United Nations is a classic case of diplomacy by deception
JOHN COLEMAN
DIPLOMACY BY DECEPTION

OMNIA VERITAS
OMNIA VERITAS LTD PRESENTS:
DRUG WAR against AMERICA
The drug trade cannot be eradicated because its directors will not allow the world's most lucrative market to be taken away from them...
BY JOHN COLEMAN
JOHN COLEMAN
DRUG WAR against AMERICA
The real promoters of this cursed trade are the "elites" of this world.

OMNIA VERITAS
OMNIA VERITAS LTD PRESENTS:
FREEMASONRY
from A to Z
by John Coleman
In the 21st century, Freemasonry has become less a secret society than a "society of secrets".
JOHN COLEMAN
FREEMASONRY from A to Z
This book explains what masonry is

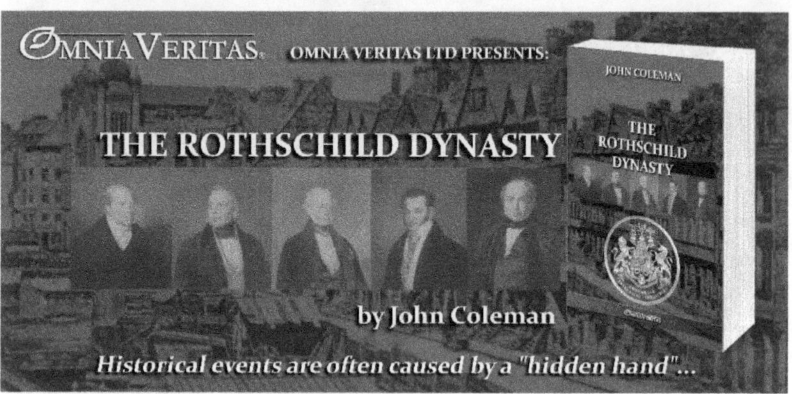
OMNIA VERITAS
OMNIA VERITAS LTD PRESENTS:
THE ROTHSCHILD DYNASTY
by John Coleman
JOHN COLEMAN
THE ROTHSCHILD DYNASTY
Historical events are often caused by a "hidden hand"...

OMNIA VERITAS
OMNIA VERITAS LTD PRESENTS:
ONE WORLD ORDER
SOCIALIST
DICTATORSHIP
All these years, while our attention was focused on the evils of communism in Moscow, the socialists in Washington were busy stealing from America!
BY JOHN COLEMAN
"The enemy in Washington is more to be feared than the enemy in Moscow."

OMNIA VERITAS
OMNIA VERITAS LTD PRESENTS :
WE FIGHT FOR OIL
BY JOHN COLEMAN
The story of the oil industry takes us into the twists and turns of "diplomacy".
The struggle to monopolize the resource coveted by all nations

OMNIA VERITAS
LIGHT-BEARERS
OF DARKNESS
This book is an attempt to show, by means of documentary evidence, that the actual world conditions are under the influence of mystic and secret societies through which the Invisible Centre is seeking to direct and dominate the nations and the world.

OMNIA VERITAS.
THE TRAIL OF THE SERPENT
An attempt to trace the worship of the ancient Serpent, the Creative Principle, the God of all initiates of the Gnostics and Cabalists, emanating from the Hellenised Jews of Alexandria.
THE TRAIL OF THE SERPENT

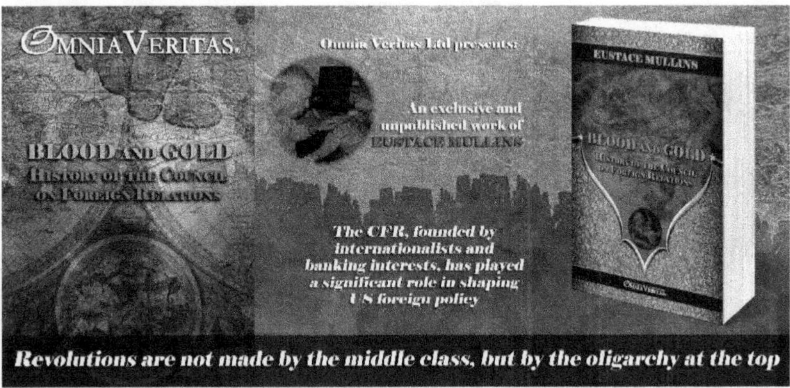
OMNIA VERITAS.
Omnia Veritas Ltd presents:
An exclusive and unpublished work of EUSTACE MULLINS
BLOOD AND GOLD
History of the Council on Foreign Relations
The CFR, founded by internationalists and banking interests, has played a significant role in shaping US foreign policy
EUSTACE MULLINS
Revolutions are not made by the middle class, but by the oligarchy at the top

OMNIA VERITAS®
www.omnia-veritas.com

www.ingramcontent.com/pod-product-compliance
Lightning Source LLC
Chambersburg PA
CBHW071123280326
41935CB00010B/1100

* 9 7 8 1 9 1 3 0 5 7 0 9 1 *